Activities Incompatible

for Tania & Nick
with best wishes

Martin

Jan 2014

By the same author

Memories of Childhood

On the Fringes of Europe: Student Years 1956-1963

Activities Incompatible

Memoirs of a Kremlinologist and a Family Man
1963-1971

Martin Nicholson

Cover image: View of the Kremlin from the British Embassy

Courtesy of Kathleen Berton Murrell

In memory of Tony Bishop and David Miller

CONTENTS

Preface

One

Kremlinology for Beginners *11*

Two

Marriage and Family *35*

Three

Moscow, 1965-1968 *59*

Four

Getting across to the Russians *101*

Five

Moscow 1971: 'Activities Incompatible' *141*

Preface

This is the third volume of my memoirs, following *Memories of Childhood* and *On the Fringes of Europe: Student Years 1956-1963*. The present volume also covers just eight years, 1963 to 1971, but they were crowded years. They encompassed the start of my work in the Research Department of the Foreign Office, two tours of duty in the Russian Secretariat at the British Embassy in Moscow, marriage and the birth of my two children.

I have enjoyed lively discussions of these years with some of my former colleagues and am grateful for the interest shown and help given by David Beattie, Christine Bishop, Philip Hanson, Ann Lewis, Caroline Miller, Geoffrey and Kathy Murrell, Roland and Katherine Smith, Marcus Wheeler and Tony Wolstenholme. How I would have loved to have similar discussions with two of my closest colleagues and friends of those years and later, Tony Bishop and David Miller. But it was not to be, and the best I can do is to dedicate this volume to their memory.

For this volume I have leant heavily on the support of my family, my wife Raili, her cousin Marjatta Sahlsten and our children Karin Weigold and Colin Nicholson. To Colin I owe a special debt of gratitude. As before, he has combined meticulous editing with searching questions. Needless to say, any remaining errors are my own responsibility.

Martin Nicholson
Twickenham
December 2013

One

Kremlinology for Beginners

This part of my story begins in the summer of 1963, early in the decade that became known as the 'Swinging Sixties'. Young people were discarding social taboos, adopting a flamboyant lifestyle and revolting against the 'establishment' in all its guises. I wasn't one of them. I was steeped in the culture of a conventional middle class family. At the age of 26, after eight years in student mode, I wanted to settle down to a career and a family of my own.

I had met my fiancée Raili Laaksonen in the little town of Hamina, Finland, where I was teaching English. Raili was a senior teacher of Swedish at the local grammar school. In Finland, teaching was a respected and well paid profession, and Raili loved it. I was without work in London once my summer job with a language school in South Kensington had come to an end. So it would have been sensible for me to join Raili in Finland and find a supporting role for myself teaching English. I did float the idea at one point when I was despairing of getting a job, but Raili, for reasons I will come to, was against it. And social convention in England, to which I was susceptible, in those days dictated that the husband's career was all-important; a working wife was expected to give up her job to start a family.

I had anyway decided that teaching English was not for me and had focused on getting into the Foreign Office as a researcher into Soviet affairs, for which I was well qualified by the standards of the day. In 1961 I had gained my degree in Russian at Cambridge University following nearly two years' intensive study of the language as a National Serviceman in the Royal Navy. I had then spent the academic year of 1961-1962 at Moscow State University with a group of British students as part of a postgraduate exchange scheme. The Foreign Office Research Department had advertised a vacancy while I was in Finland, but I had let the opportunity slip, not realising that there was a fixed number of established posts, and no further vacancies would come up until an existing member of the small cadre of researchers either retired or left. I was not too discouraged, however, as I had inside information that temporary posts came up from time to time when, for example, one of the cadre was posted to Moscow. My insiders were George Walden, who had been with me at Cambridge and Moscow, and Tony Bishop, my contemporary on the Services course and at Cambridge, and whose career was to be intimately linked to mine. They secured me an interview with their boss, the Head of Soviet Section, Research Department, who exercised considerable powers of patronage.

He was the redoubtable Ted Orchard, the doyen of British government experts on the Soviet Union. Ted could boast of postings to the British Embassy in Moscow from 1948 onwards, on top of an Oxford degree and a couple of years lecturing at the university. He was respected in the international Russia-watching community and well known as an eccentric figure around Whitehall. His appearance, somewhat dishevelled, with a long, usually unkempt beard, was totally at odds with the fashion of the time among civil servants in London. It made him a conspicuous figure in Moscow as well, where, it was said, he was sometimes mistaken for a Russian Orthodox priest in mufti, or even as the reincarnation of the infamous monk Rasputin, who had cast a fatal spell on the family of the last Russian tsar. Ted himself liked to tell the story of an episode at a public swimming pool in the centre of Moscow that had been built on the site of a former cathedral and was popularly supposed to be haunted by the ghosts of priests: on seeing Ted surfacing from the depths, a panic-stricken Russian swimmer instinctively crossed himself. When Ted went to Moscow to interpret for British political leaders, the Soviet Foreign Minister Gromyko liked to joke that he was 'your Fidel Castro'.

This was the figure I was brought in to see. I don't know what impression I made on him at that first interview, or indeed how much of me he could see at all, as he was seated at his desk behind a large barricade of books and canvas bags, unsorted after a move to a new office. For my part, I saw nothing but a bearded, thickly bespectacled head occasionally peering suspiciously out from behind the ramparts and muttering a few delphic remarks before withdrawing again. But the outcome was clear. There would be no vacancies for the foreseeable future.

The sage of Haslemere: Ted Orchard in later years.

A discreet, white-collar Labour Exchange (as Job Centres were then called) in London led me to two other interviews with government bodies, both unproductive. One was with the Information Research

Department of the Foreign Office, a little-publicised department whose job it was to counter Soviet propaganda in the Third World. The other was at Leconfield House in Curzon Street, where I was grilled by two steely-eyed men and emerged with the feeling that they had learnt every detail of my past life, while I was still unsure even of what job I was applying for. It was 'classified', I had been told. Only years later did I realise that I had been in the headquarters of the Security Service, popularly known as MI5. When they heard that my real interest was in joining the Foreign Office, they lost interest: 'We don't poach from other government departments,' they said, primly.

My fortunes turned when I shared my frustrations with Andrew Bache, my contemporary from Cambridge and flatmate in Earls Court Square. Already well ensconced in the Commonwealth Relations Office, at that time still a separate department of state from the Foreign Office, Andrew was familiar with the ways of the Civil Service and was aghast that my fate seemed to depend on a mere section head in a department. There was a proper procedure for recruiting people through Personnel Department. Andrew gave me the details, and in due course I had an interview with an official there.

The official again said that I should wait till a vacancy was advertised. In the meantime I could talk to the Director of Research, R W Mason. He was expecting me and to my astonishment promptly asked me when I wanted to start work. So as not to appear over-eager I invented a couple of competing engagements and suggested a day towards the end of October 1963. Mr Mason continued to warn me that this was only a temporary appointment and that it carried no guarantee of transfer to an established post, for which I would have to apply in the usual way, if and when one came up. I wasn't worried: my foot was in the door, and I had a feeling it wouldn't be removed. Nor was it, until I left on retirement 34 years later.

Research Department was not a standard Foreign Office department. Its origins lay in Oxford, not Whitehall: it was the brainchild of the historian Professor Arnold Toynbee.[1] Towards the end of the First World War Toynbee had been a member of the short-lived Political Intelligence Department of the Foreign Office, and as war clouds gathered again in 1938 he secured Foreign Office backing to set up the Foreign Research and Press Service (FRPS) in Balliol College, Oxford. The aim of the FRPS was to provide the government with accurate information on foreign affairs at a critical time. Toynbee brought to Oxford the press cuttings library and some of the staff from the Royal Institute of International Affairs in London, better known as Chatham House, where he was Director of Studies, and added a wealth of academic talent from Oxford itself. The FRPS quickly gained recognition, so much so that by 1942 its distance

---

[1] The department's official history has been written by two of my colleagues, the late Bob Longmire (from whom I took over in Moscow in 1971) and Ken Walker from China Section. Robert A Longmire and Kenneth C Walker, *Herald of a noisy world – interpreting the news of all the nations, The Research and Analysis Department of the Foreign and Commonwealth Office, A History*, FCO Foreign Policy Document (Special Issue) No 263, 1995

from London and its unofficial status came to be seen as serious disadvantages. It was moved to the capital and formally established as the Foreign Office Research Department (FORD) in April 1943, with Toynbee as its director. The assumption was, however, that the Department would be wound up at the end of the war, and for this reason the staff were classed as temporary civil servants. In the event, the need for serious analysis of international affairs was as great after the war as before; the department was retained and its staff eventually became established civil servants.

FORD was initially based in Cornwall House, near Waterloo Station, but its corporate identity as a department was weak. Individual sections of FORD gravitated towards the geographical departments of the Foreign Office to whose demands for information they responded. Soviet Section was the first to move. In 1954 the section crossed the Thames to Whitehall in order to be nearer the department responsible for policy towards the Soviet Union, which at that time was called Northern Department. The department wanted experts on tap to give depth to its policy recommendations during a critical period. The communist, totalitarian Soviet Union and its satellites in Eastern Europe were pitted against the capitalist, democratic West under the leadership of the United States. This was what came to be known as the Cold War.

I was not thinking about the bigger issues on 21st October 1963 when I stepped into the old India Office to start work. The goals may have been lofty and the location prestigious, but the work was humdrum and conditions basic. I shared a large room with some six or seven others – it was hard to know how many as they were all virtually hidden under piles of books, papers and filing boxes, much as Ted Orchard had been when he interviewed me.

At one point I had a desk next to the floor-to-ceiling window overlooking Durbar Court. The courtyard has now been restored to its original glory and is the resplendent venue for public events. At that time it was a neglected space with just one wooden shack in the middle – the telegram distribution centre. There was ample access for birds, including pigeons, who found the wide ledges ideal for nest building. In the spring I waged a war of attrition with one pair, who were building their home just a foot from where I sat. Every morning I would prise open the huge window and kick their collection of sticks off the ledge to join the general mess in the courtyard below. But they had set their hearts on this location and patiently rebuilt overnight what I had destroyed. And they had one advantage over me: I worked a five-day week; they worked all seven days. After the long Easter weekend I arrived to find the nest rebuilt once again, and this time with eggs in it. I didn't have the heart to kick that lot over the edge.

It was nearly as filthy indoors as out, surrounded as we were by piles of low quality Soviet newsprint that spread excess ink on everything it came into contact with. Convention demanded that I went to work in a suit and white shirt. The shirt ended the day grey with ink. Back numbers of our Soviet papers were stored in boxes, where they gradually disintegrated. Open coal fires, topped up occasionally by incongruously frock-coated messengers, completed the Dickensian picture.

The piles of Soviet newspapers were inescapable: they were our bread and butter. We read and analysed them in the hope of finding nuggets of information that would help to reveal what was happening the Soviet Union. This was seldom what its leaders would have us believe. Our work was always difficult to explain outside the office, and even to some people inside the office. It could be seen as either sinister – the 'dark art' of reading between the lines of the Communist Party newspaper *Pravda* – or just silly, poring over group photos of the Soviet leadership to see who was on the way up and who was on the way down.

The Politburo in 1979: we knew them all.
www.davno.ru

In fact, we were engaged in the entirely normal and legitimate exercise of political analysis – finding out how power was exercised, who was exercising it and to what ends. The 'dark art' was practised not by us but by the Soviet leaders themselves. They were unable to tell the truth about how they ruled without revealing the hollowness of their claim to have invented an entirely new and advanced form of society. The claim was that the Soviet Union was the first country in the world where the working masses, whose labour had previously created wealth for the benefit of the ruling classes, now actually enjoyed the fruits of their toil. A pyramid of workers' councils ('soviets' in Russian, hence the name of the country) from local soviets to the Supreme Soviet at the top – the country's parliament – was allegedly the vehicle through which the workers exercised their new-found power. Their goal was Communism, an ideal state where each would freely give what they could and receive what they needed, an example that would be followed, in time, throughout the world.

The Supreme Soviet was in fact nothing but a 'rubber stamp' parliament. It convened only once or twice a year to approve the policies of the Communist Party, which had seized power in the Russian Revolution of 1917 and now claimed to be the force that had opened the way for the humble worker and peasant parliamentary deputies to enter the glittering halls of the Kremlin with their heads held high. Congresses of the Supreme Soviet were the occasion for Moscow to be invaded by high-achieving steelworkers, miners and milkmaids, together with colourfully attired representatives of the national minorities from the fringes of the vast empire, as if on a holiday outing. My late colleague David Miller once found himself in the same hotel as a young deputy from the provinces, in Moscow for her first Congress. She was completely bemused about why she was there and grateful for the briefing that this foreign expert was able to give her.

The justification for this state of affairs was that whilst the workers and peasants knew what their aspirations were, they could not be expected to know how to achieve them, being largely untutored. So they had delegated this responsibility to the brightest and best among them, the leaders of the Communist Party, who understood that the wheel of history was inevitably turning towards socialism and communism, but also knew when and how it needed to be nudged forward. The Communist Party leaders were themselves guided by two beacons. The first was Karl Marx, the German political economist who in the nineteenth century had elaborated the theory of Communism: a society of equals that would free the working class from the chains that bound them to their bosses. The second was Vladimir Lenin, the Russian revolutionary who had developed the theory and practice of how to seize power from an exploiting class that would never willingly give it up.

Marx and Lenin wove a dense web of philosophy and political theory, but both acknowledged that their theorising was a means to an end – power. Lenin summed up it all up in two Russian words, *kto kogo*, 'Who whom' or 'Who holds the whip hand'.

Lenin held the whip hand while he was alive, but he failed to indicate before dying in 1924 who among his fellow rulers should inherit it. With no agreed rules to go by, Lenin's successors embarked on a struggle for power within the ruling Communist Party that continued throughout the life of the Soviet Union itself. It was conducted in secret. Many of the Party's revolutionary leaders had spent time in Tsarist prisons and in exile, from where they had hatched their plot to overthrow the old regime. Their world was one of conspiracy and a morbid fear of informers and traitors.

Joseph Dzhugashvili, a native of Georgia in the Caucasus, who had adopted the *nom de guerre* of Stalin ('man of steel'), won the first major power struggle. Unprepossessing and with heavily accented Russian, Stalin in public was no match for the flaming oratory and revolutionary *élan* of his better known colleagues. But even while Lenin was alive Stalin had understood that the important thing was to get his hands on the levers of power and had worked himself into what was then the modest position of the Party's General Secretary. Over a quarter of a century, until his death in 1953, he used his skills to build himself a position of absolute power. But he felt secure only when he had ruthlessly eliminated all real and supposed opponents, including the most talented politicians, soldiers, scientists and artists of his generation. Absurdly, he carried out his purges in the name of 'scientific Marxism-Leninism', to which he added 'Stalinism'. His word on every subject from economics to linguistics became law, and woe betide anyone who failed to follow every twist of his thinking. Stalin's line was the

Party's line. The Party's line was 'scientific' and therefore correct. It followed that when Stalin abruptly changed or reversed a policy, the previous policy had to be expunged from the record, along with those officials who had espoused it. They were sent to the *gulag* or to their deaths and their images crudely cut out of photographs where they had once stood proudly among the leadership.

A similar fate befell Stalin himself after his death in 1953. It was a gradual process, which reached its climax in late 1961 when the new Party leader Nikita Khrushchev had gathered sufficient power in his own hands safely to consign Stalin to the realms of 'non-people'. I had been a student in Moscow when Stalin's mummified body was removed from its position of honour next to Lenin's in the mausoleum on Red Square and I had watched as his gigantic portraits in the metro stations turned one by one into plain, whitewashed walls.

Khrushchev was not another Stalin, and his defeated opponents rarely suffered more than loss of position and privilege. But it was just as vital for officials to know – and if possible anticipate – their leader's abrupt changes of mood and policy and to associate themselves with those of his circle who were on their way up, not down. Anyone who wanted to succeed in the system had to be able to read the signs that were indirectly purveyed in speeches, in appointments and dismissals, and in press articles. Alexander Solzhenitsyn, the celebrated Soviet writer and Nobel Prize winner, described the process through the eyes of the anti-hero of his novel *Cancer Ward*, the Party bureaucrat Pavel Rusanov:

[Rusanov] was wildly jealous if someone else, uninitiated, got his fingers on the daily newspaper before he did. None of them here [in the cancer ward] could possibly understand what he understood in the newspaper. He regarded the paper as an instruction, distributed openly, but actually written in code. It was an instruction in which not everything could be stated directly, but where a skilful and knowledgeable man could piece together through various small hints – the arrangement of the articles, the things that were *not* said, or omitted – a reliable picture of the latest policy line. This was why Rusanov *had* to read the paper first.

This was our job in Research Department too, to find the message hidden in the jargon. Happily, our lives didn't depend on it, and we were able to enjoy the light relief offered by the sillier items. One of my favourites was the 'un-personing' of Stalin's erstwhile security chief Lavrentii Beria, who had wielded such power that the rest of Stalin's successors in the political leadership only felt safe after they had had him shot in 1953, accusing him among other things of working for British intelligence. Unfortunately for the keepers of the ever-changing historical record, a newly-minted volume of the official Soviet encyclopaedia containing a three page eulogy of Beria had just been printed and distributed. Together with their copy of the new volume, subscribers to the encyclopaedia (including us in Soviet Section) were sent instructions to cut out and destroy the offending pages and replace them with three new pages, which contained no mention of Beria at all, but included instead a space-filling article on the Bering Sea. We dutifully inserted the three new pages, but being far from the Kremlin's watchful eye we didn't destroy the article on Beria.

Soviet newspapers and journals were not the only material that came our way. The BBC Monitoring Service, based in Caversham Park, near Reading, listened to radio broadcasts around the world, translated them, summarised them and by the end of each day had produced four colour-coded *Summaries of World Broadcasts* (known in the trade as SWBs): green for the Far East; ochre for the Middle East; blue for Eastern Europe; and red, appropriately, for the Soviet Union. These were bread and butter for journalists as well as diplomats and had the advantage of speed (our Soviet papers might arrive a week or so late) and coverage of regional broadcasts that we would otherwise miss altogether, as our access to the Soviet regional press was limited.

Together, these made up our 'unclassified' sources, that is, they were publicly available. Other sources were 'classified', which meant simply that they were classed as Restricted, Confidential, Secret or Top Secret, the choice of classification being left to the originator of the report. Two or three times a day a stack of diplomatic telegrams, mostly Restricted or Confidential, would issue from the grimy little hut under my window on to our desks. We were on the distribution list of diplomatic reporting not only from the British Embassy in Moscow, but from any post where the Soviet Union was involved. I devoured them eagerly, as much to increase my general knowledge as to find items of direct relevance to whatever subject I happened to be working on at the time. Then we had intelligence material. There were reports from the Secret Intelligence Service, or MI6 as it is more commonly called, which came in distinctive Red Jackets (RJs). They provided spice for researchers like me to offset our stodgy diet of the Soviet press, while we provided the perspective gained from close study of the open sources – a form of 'reality check'. In his Cold War espionage novel *Tinker, Tailor, Soldier, Spy*, John Le Carré credits a fictitious member of Foreign Office Research Department with finding discrepancies in a series of intelligence reports significant enough to cast doubt on their authenticity, for which he is told to mind his own business. I'm glad to say that in real life our comments were rather better received. Finally, there were Blue Jackets (BJs), which enclosed material from Government Communications Headquarters (GCHQ) in Cheltenham. They were only available to those who after some years of service were deemed secure enough to be 'indoctrinated', that is, officially made aware of the government's practice of eavesdropping on international signals traffic. So although I knew about them, initially I was not allowed to read them.

Working in an office was a new experience for me. True, before going to Cambridge I had had a holiday job as a messenger in the headquarters of Shell in the City and indeed saw my own father there, seated solemnly at his desk between his 'IN' and 'OUT' trays, looking very different from the Dad I knew at home. Now here I was between my own trays, and I was told that my job was to read the stuff that came into my IN tray, highlight passages that might be significant, mark the pieces to an appropriate file and put them in the OUT tray. For someone who had found teaching stressful, this quiet and steady work was bliss. At the same time it was monotonous and would have been dispiriting but for two factors.

The first was the company in which I found myself. We were a closely knit group of boffins without any ambitions in the traditional sense – there was no career advancement to be had in Research Department beyond going up a grade every so often. Our satisfaction derived entirely from our work, and since much of that was narrow and tedious, it came to life only when we were able to share the results of our research with each other. I had immediately felt at home in this atmosphere, which was co-operative rather than competitive. I already knew some of my colleagues. Of the two 'insiders' who had introduced me to the job, Tony Bishop was by now on a posting to Moscow, but George Walden was still there and acted as my mentor. I also knew Marcus Wheeler, who had been at the Moscow Embassy when I was a student in Moscow and would go on to an academic career culminating in the chair of Russian at Queen's University Belfast, and Geoff Murrell, who had also been in the Embassy and with whom I would 'cox and box' throughout my career. My initial passage was further eased by the departure of Ted Orchard for Moscow. In his place as Head of Soviet Section sat the more approachable figure of Eddie Bolland, who had just come back from a Moscow posting and who many years later was to be my ambassador in Vienna. Eddie was just keeping the seat warm for Ted, who seemed to have proprietorial rights to it. A generalist diplomat, not a researcher, Eddie knew more than Ted about the arcane ways of the Foreign Office and was a better person to have as my first boss.

The other factor to alleviate the monotony of our work lay in the knowledge that it was appreciated, in particular by our immediate patrons, the desk officers of Northern Department. They were the principal commissioners and readers of our research papers and minutes, the people who would ring up for a quick briefing on some obscure topic and who would search our collective memory. They were different animals to us – Branch A diplomats, the high-flyers. We researchers belonged to Branch B, which included all the lesser fry. But many of these high-flyers had worked alongside researchers from Soviet Section in the Moscow Embassy, which was a great leveller, and they had learnt the value of the solid knowledge of the inner workings of the Soviet system that we provided. I had already met two of them during my time in Moscow as a student – Christopher Mallaby, who would go on to become Ambassador to Germany and France, and Anthony Loehnis, who had given me Christmas lunch in Moscow in 1961. Anthony was a diplomat in the classic mode, with a studied air of *insouciance* that concealed an acute mind. A deceptive amateurism was the style of the times. When I left the Diplomatic Service 34 years later the style had changed – busy-ness was the order of the day, however trivial the matter in hand.

I was a natural 'back room boy', with a consuming interest in things Russian and little interest in the art of diplomacy as such. I had no thought of trying to join the high-flyers, although I made a couple of attempts later in my career, driven by circumstance more than ambition. By contrast, George Walden's restless and searching intellect would not be contained within the framework of Soviet affairs. He widened his brief to include the ideological dispute between the Soviet Union and China as they competed for leadership of the world Communist movement, became a China expert and finally transferred to Branch A, where he shone, before becoming an MP. George tried to persuade me to do something similar if I were not to end up as an expert in some facet of Soviet internal politics, knowing more and more about less and less – a dead end in his view. But having always felt most comfortable when I knew the boundaries to what I was expected to understand, that was precisely what I was drawn to. I volunteered for a routine job helping to maintain the card index of Soviet personalities – our own *Who's Who* of the Soviet Union.

The so-called Personalities Room, where the index was kept, was the engine room of Soviet Section. Down the middle was a long double row of metal cabinets holding thousands of index cards. Around these cabinets sat half a dozen indexers, combing the newspapers and any other documents that came their way and making entries on the cards of relevant individuals. They included indexers on loan from MI6, which had no comparable resource of its own and valued ours. Other members of the section would come in to check the cards of personalities relevant to the research they were doing and to create their own entries from the material they had. Thus the total number of cards increased by the day. Eventually it reached a point where worried structural engineers forced us to line the cabinets up against load bearing walls in case the whole lot fell through the floor. I was an enthusiastic advocate of computerising these records when it first became a practical possibility, a decade or so after I had started work. But the computer expert was cautious: if you're comfortable with your present method, don't change it, he advised. How right he was. Not only were we saved from what would have turned out to be a very primitive form of database, but we were able to preserve the individuality of the handwritten entries in this unique compendium.

I was set to work on the Soviet leadership – the Politburo and the Secretariat of the Communist Party. Its members were the monochrome figures – some 15 to 20 of them – who lined up twice a year in near identical Homburg hats and shapeless coats on top of Lenin's mausoleum to take the salute: solemnly on the national day of 7th November as tanks and rocket launchers trundled through Red Square; and with a touch more levity on 1st May as the populace filed past carrying floats demonstrating their achievements, together with icons of the distant leaders they were saluting. The leaders were monochrome because they had subordinated their individuality to the principle of collective leadership, which lay at the heart of the rule of the 'proletariat'. The principle was consistently flouted by the one who had scrambled to the top of the pile – Lenin, Stalin and now the flamboyant Khrushchev. But apart from the acknowledged leader of the day, everything was done to conceal the relative political weight, or even the job, of the other members of the leadership, not to mention their personalities. It was up to others, including us Kremlinologists, to find out who did what and who wielded most power.

My contribution was to compile an unexciting but essential reference document called *The Interlocking Party and Government Leadership of the USSR*. This showed how officials of the Communist Party apparatus dominated the governmental decision-making process. By contrast, only a few members of the government, parliament and sometimes military, made it to the Communist Party's all-important Politburo. Without my modest document to hand it was hard for our senior officials to convince a British cabinet minister that his opposite number in the Soviet government was little more than a civil servant if he was not a member of the Party's policy-making inner sanctum. At that time not even the long-serving Soviet Foreign Minister Andrei Gromyko was a member of the Politburo. Policy, including foreign policy, was made by party secretaries, well out of the public eye.

The secrecy with which the party leaders operated was the reason for my other routine but necessary work. I logged all public appearances, day by day, of the leadership. Only by recording over a matter of years which meetings they attended and whose obituaries they signed could we build up a picture of which party secretary did what, particularly in the sensitive areas of defence and security. We also learnt to understand their work and leisure routines. Sometimes members of the leadership failed to appear for weeks or months on end, and then the hue and cry would be raised among Western Kremlin-watchers – was so-and-so in disgrace or dead? As often as not they were just on holiday – a spell at an elite sanatorium by the Black Sea was one of the privileges of office. We developed a good idea of who took their holiday when, so were able to dampen the fires of speculation that were fuelled more by our senior officials and ministers than by us Kremlinologists. 'Why do they want to know?' I asked someone in Northern Department as I grumbled about having to write an analysis of the non-appearance of some junior member of the leadership. 'Leaders are fascinated by other leaders,' was the laconic reply.

Taking a holiday on the Black Sea was a privilege that carried risks, however, as it gave your rivals the chance to plot behind your back. On 12th October 1964, while on a late holiday, Khrushchev was summoned to Moscow by his colleagues in the leadership to be told that his time was up. The other Party leaders, who had only a few weeks previously praised him for his wisdom, now accused him of being rude and unpredictable, and of pursuing reforms that 'contradicted Lenin's teaching'. Khrushchev, who had won so many power struggles, finally gave in and resigned.

At the time we didn't know the details of the accusations, but could easily deduce them from the phrases that appeared in a *Pravda* editorial without actually naming Khrushchev: 'Subjectivism and drift ... harebrained scheming ... half-baked conclusions ... bragging and bluster, attraction to rule by fiat' and so on. Khrushchev had accumulated too much power. He wore the two most powerful 'hats' in the leadership – First Secretary of the Party's Central Committee and Chairman of the Council of Ministers, or Prime Minister. The leadership resolved in future not to allow these two posts to be held by one man.

So with Khrushchev gone, two men emerged – the new Party leader Leonid Brezhnev and the new Prime Minister Aleksei Kosygin. They were another 'B & K', reminiscent of the B & K (Nikolai Bulganin as Prime Minister and Khrushchev as Party Leader) who had visited the UK in tandem in 1956. As Prime Minister, Bulganin had been nominally the leader of the delegation, but Khrushchev was the more powerful, and two years later had taken over Bulganin's post himself. Who of the new 'B & K' would come out on top? The course of the new power struggle would absorb us for the next decade or so.

The new Soviet leadership might have used the occasion to set some limit on a leader's term of office, but they let the opportunity slip. The reasons given for the still vigorous 70-year-old Khrushchev's resignation – advanced age and deteriorating health – were transparently false (he lived for another eight years). The next three leaders, however, all continued in office till they died in their early to mid 70s, genuinely old and sick. The system's ability to reform and reinvigorate itself was thus circumscribed from as early as 1964. As the Soviet Union was increasing its standing as a world power, internal decay was already eating away at its innards.

With my fellow analysts I followed this process on and off right up to the Soviet Union's collapse in 1991. But in the autumn of 1964 I had more pressing concerns. Raili and I had married in the summer and we were expecting our first child.

Two

Marriage and Family

R aili had arrived at Tilbury, the principal port for London, on Sunday 14th June 1964, just three days before we were due to be married. She was aboard the *Baltika*, one of the Soviet steamships that plied the route between London and Leningrad, as St Petersburg was then called, stopping off at Nordic ports on the way. The very same ship had taken me to the Soviet Union to begin my postgraduate year at Moscow University in September 1961 and again to Helsinki in October 1962 to start my year of teaching in Finland.

Apart from this tenuous link, the year in Finland had had nothing to do with my involvement in the Soviet Union. In the summer of 1962, uncertain of what to do after Moscow University, I had mentioned to the British Council an interest in teaching English to foreigners. They had recommended me to try it out: there was a vacant slot among the 30-odd teachers they sent to Finland every year. So in October I had arrived in the little town of Hamina. It was a mere 40 kilometres (25 miles) from the Soviet border, but here I felt as far away from Russia as I did in England, or perhaps further, as the Finns at that time pointedly ignored the 'big neighbour' with whom they shared the longest common border in Europe. They had enjoyed less than 50 years of independence from Russia and had come close to losing it when forced to sue for peace towards the end of the Second World War – Finland had fought alongside the Germans in a vain attempt to regain territories ceded to the Soviet Union after the latter's invasion of Finland in 1939. *Ruki vverkh!* – 'Hands up!' – was about all the Russian most Finns of my acquaintance knew or wanted to know. For despite their reversals, the Finns were proud of having defended and retained their independence, their own democratic institutions and their own way of life, unlike the countries of Eastern Europe that had been forced after the war into the Soviet orbit. Although the Finnish government took care not to offend the Soviet Union (it refused to condemn even the Soviet invasion of Hungary in 1956), in outlook the Finnish people were firmly oriented towards the West. One of the British Council's contributions to keeping them that way was the teaching programme of which I was now part.

Raili had been among a group of teachers in a class I ran. She and I got along well, and she became my mentor and friend as I got to know Finland. Two years older than me and well established in her career, she was the senior partner in Hamina. The idea of marrying never occurred to us, despite others seeing it a long way off. Only when Raili visited England in the summer of 1963 and saw me on my home ground did the balance of our relationship change. And only after she had left did I propose marriage – by letter.

It was easier for me to propose than for Raili to respond: in coming to a decision she had more issues to address than I did. Having made a written list of the pros and cons and consulted her father, to whom she was close, she decided that she did want to marry me, move to England and start a family, although this would mean abandoning her parents, the work she loved, and indeed her homeland. The idea of living in Finland as a married couple was as difficult for her as it was for me. She didn't much like her Hamina *persona*. It had been a difficult period: she was coming to terms with her Finnish fiancé of two years breaking off their engagement; and she was meeting the challenge of looking after her teenage cousin Marjatta, who had recently lost her mother and was sharing Raili's flat. Raili didn't want to be the dominant partner in our marriage, as inevitably she would be if we lived in Finland. She wanted to re-mould herself as a loving wife and mother in the country where she had seen in my family an example of how to do it. Warwick Lodge, our family home in St Margaret's (Twickenham), where Raili had been made so welcome that summer, was the model she wanted to emulate.

Once we had settled on our course, our commitment never wavered. But we only saw each other twice before our marriage in June 1964. Communication throughout our long engagement – a whole academic year – was almost exclusively by letter. As autumn turned to winter in Finland, Raili's Nordic introspection often tested my patience, while my persistent anxiety about how I would provide for her in England tested hers. In Hamina our relationship had been carefree and easy, partly because we had never had to make any serious decisions together. Now suddenly we were planning to marry and settle down in what was for Raili a foreign country. I was unused to Raili's habit of throwing out ideas as they occurred to her and took her suggestions far too literally, especially when she was musing about how we might live in England.

Raili's living conditions in Hamina were comfortable – she owned an elegant, modern flat, furnished in the minimalist, Scandinavian style that we both admired. Would I be able to provide anything comparable in England? Even when I did finally get my Foreign Office job, the salary of £914 per annum (roughly equivalent to £15,000 50 years later) was modest. Raili would save us money by bringing over her own furniture, but this was a mixed blessing: it more or less ruled out our renting rather than buying, since in those days the practice was to let houses furnished.

Consumed by these anxieties, I was not at my best when Raili came over for our official engagement. For my father's sake I put an announcement in *The Times* on Christmas Eve, 1963. To give it a slightly exotic feel I used the Finnish *Neiti* (Miss) as Raili's title. This was an insult, as the Finns attach great importance to academic qualifications, and no one with a degree, as Raili had, could be a plain 'miss'. *Maisteri* (Master of Arts) would have been the correct title. Raili bore it without complaint, but when it came to practical matters she was more forthright. She recoiled from a terraced house at the far end of Twickenham that I took her to see as an example of what we might be able to afford: it was a dark warren of small rooms in a state which turned both our stomachs. Not that Raili was unfamiliar with poor quality housing in England – ten years previously she had spent a summer as an *au pair* with a Latvian immigrant family in Doncaster – but she had raised her sights somewhat on experiencing my family home.

So after Raili had returned to Finland I looked for lighter, brighter houses in more rural surroundings. I quickly rejected a terraced house near Egham that had been advertised as bordering a lake – it turned out to be an uninspiring reservoir. But I fell for the picturesque Bishop's Farm Cottage in Oakley Green on the edge of Windsor Great Park. I thought Raili would enjoy the surroundings, even if it meant condemning her to social isolation and me to a four-mile journey even to begin my commute from Windsor Station. In mid-January I went so far as to make an offer of £3,850, subject to survey. Thank goodness for that condition! The surveyor's damning report concluded:

'... quite frankly, we are a little disturbed as to whether or not
you should proceed with your proposed purchase. The type of
structure is such that it would almost appear that the building was
originally a store shed to which a lean-to was added and the
whole converted to form living accommodation.'

The surveyor even rang me one evening to go further than he had felt able to do in his written report. His message was: don't buy this shack!

In that frenzied month Raili was thinking up ever more imaginative ways of soaking up the Finnmarks she thought she would earn from the sale of her flat (forgetting for a moment that she had borrowed the money from her father) and thus helping me out of my dilemma. She even suggested that I buy the plot of land while she bought the component parts of a prefabricated Finnish house and shipped them over. The idea of a Finnish log cabin effortlessly settling on a countryside plot, fully connected to all utilities, must have disposed of the rural idyll for good. At all events, by mid-February I had bought something altogether more conventional: a ground floor flat on the road that led from Twickenham Green towards the river Thames and Hampton Court. It was close to as much water and greenery as you could wish for in the London suburbs, and it was only 15 minutes by bus from my family home, where my parents were to provide Raili as a newcomer to the country with much appreciated support. 86 Hampton Road was a large, Victorian house that had recently been converted by Waites, the construction company, whose 'Waites houses' across the river in Ham were attracting attention by their modern design and building methods. Flat 2 had two spacious rooms, one with a partitioned kitchen area. I provided just one piece of furniture, an enormous wardrobe bought for the knock-down price of £11 at our local antique dealer, Phelps. I placed it with its back to the room so that as well as storing our entire collection of clothes it formed a neat little dressing room. I covered the unsightly back with wallpaper painted brilliant white to match the rest of the decor. My father, ever the practical carpenter, built a space-saving round dining table with a central leg, while Raili later provided the rest of the furniture, shipped in a container from her flat in Hamina. The flat was ideal for us, and I snapped it up by paying the required £3,450 in cash with a bridging loan from my father's bank. Unfortunately I had made only the vaguest enquiries about how to turn the bridging loan into a mortgage. I learnt too late that no mortgage company would look seriously at this sort of conversion – its physical boundaries and the terms of the leasehold were just too vaguely defined – so now it was my turn to borrow from my father.

Over Easter 1964 I visited Finland to meet Raili's parents for the first time and see the parish of Artjärvi, in the south of Finland, where she came from. I say 'parish' advisedly, as it was neither village nor town. Originally a conglomeration of farms built tightly together as a defence against wolves and bears, it had over time spread to encompass many large, remote farmsteads, and it had no clearly defined centre. Raili's parents were country people, but not farmers. Nor were they natives of Artjärvi. Her father Väinö Laaksonen was from Loviisa, on the coast some 45 kilometres (28 miles) south of Artjärvi. Väinö's own father had indeed been the son of a farmer, but, significantly, he was not the eldest son. Finnish society worked on the principle that the first son inherited the whole

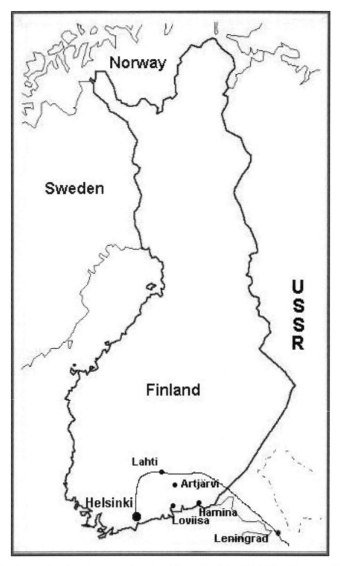

Finland: map showing places mentioned and the route of the Helsinki to Moscow railway

farm, whilst the others had to find some other way of making their living. This was to avoid land being split into ever smaller parcels. Väinö's father had become a carpenter. Väinö himself, born in 1905, had left school at 14 to start work in Loviisa as an office boy with the local electricity company, *Kymenlaakson Sähkö*. It took its name from the valley of the river *Kymi*, up which it gradually spread its network and where the young Väinö began work in the field as an electrician, having completed evening classes at the local technical college. That was as far as the family finances would allow his education to go, to his lasting regret, as he had a thirst for knowledge. He had met Alli Petäjä, the daughter of another carpenter, while working in a neighbouring parish, and they married in 1934, just a year after my parents. Raili was born in 1935, and two years later Väinö was appointed manager of the company's branch in Artjärvi, where he stayed for the next 40 years. Artjärvi was just 30 kilometres (20 miles) from Alli's home, but the distance was enough in those days for the locals to speak a different dialect, and Raili's mother never quite lost the feeling that Artjärvi wasn't 'home'.

Like me, Raili was brought up in a secure and loving family, but unlike me she was an only child and had to find her friends outside the home. The happiest memories from her early years centre on the *Kirkonmäki* – the hill that led from her parents' house up to the church – and the group of children she played with there, some of whom she is still in touch with today. The focus then shifted to her local primary school (after a long, frustrating wait, since Finnish children only start school at the age of seven), and finally away from home altogether in term-time while at grammar school in Loviisa – there being no school at that level in Artjärvi. In Loviisa she lived with her father's brother and his wife, who had no children of their own. In theory she came home at weekends, but she often forgot, as life was much more exciting with her friends in Loviisa.

The Artjärvi office of *Kymenlaakson Sähkö* was also the Laaksonen home, so Raili's father didn't go out to work. He was responsible for planning and running the entire electricity network of the area. His workforce would appear in the morning to get their instructions for the day – this telegraph pole needed fixing, that transformer needed checking – and reappear after work. The office and home also served as the shop where people could buy electrical spares – bulbs, fuses and so on – and later have their televisions repaired, so there was a steady stream of visitors, which Raili's sociable mother enjoyed and which contributed to Raili's outgoing manner and ease with strangers – not characteristic of Finns of her time.

Probably the first visitor I met on my Easter stay, and certainly the one I remember, was Toivo Koivu, a small, dapper man with a twinkle in his eye, who lived just across the road and appeared one morning with a jar of honey in one hand and the day's post in the other. The honey he had made himself and was selling locally, the post he was delivering because it was his week to do so – the job was shared out among the local householders. *Koivunsetä* (Uncle Koivu) as Raili had always called him, did several jobs: he was a barber and a skilled tailor, making for the local men a strong but handsome twill suit (called *diagonaalipuku* on account of its diagonal weave) whose ankle-length breeches fitted into the boots that were essential wear in the Finnish countryside. He and his family were also the core of a local band that played at the Saturday evening dances, while his son Jaakko provided the local taxi service. This was a self-help community, and the Laaksonen household was one of its hubs.

My poor Finnish limited communication with Raili's parents, but they made it clear that they welcomed me and fully accepted my going off with their only child. In Hamina the attitude was a shade less generous. Apart from her close friends and her headmaster, to whom she had had to give her notice, Raili had kept her marriage plans to herself until she returned from her Christmas visit to the UK, displaying her diamond engagement ring (an inheritance from my great aunt). Although there were many who congratulated her, some of Raili's colleagues were angry that she was prepared to abandon both school and country. The local pastor put an aggravating bureaucratic obstacle in our way. Although not a churchgoer, like most Finns Raili was officially a member of the Lutheran church, which kept a record of all the major events in her life, civil as well as religious, and whose authority was needed for Raili to apply for a passport stating she was leaving the country on marriage. The pastor refused to provide Raili with the necessary certificate unless she produced a document proving that her husband-to-be wasn't already married. I vaguely recall a rather unpleasant interview with him during the Easter visit, in which I tried in vain to explain that I couldn't prove a negative under English law; the best I could come up with was a Certificate of No Impediment to Marriage, issued after banns had been posted and aroused no objections. Had we been intending to get married in Finland the pastor's obstinacy might have presented us with a real problem, but as it was, Raili simply by-passed him by getting an ordinary passport as if she were going on holiday.

Raili's lonely four-day journey on the *Baltika* had given her plenty of time to be sad about all she was leaving and apprehensive about all that lay ahead, but there was little time for further reflection once she arrived, as three days later we were parading at the Register Office for our civil wedding. We had decided to get married quietly in England – the cultural divide was just too great for a full scale wedding in either of our countries. So at Christmas we had approached Robert Patkai, the pastor of St John's Lutheran Church in Collingham Gardens, Kensington, not far from the Earl's Court Square flat where I was then living, who was enthusiastic. Most of his congregation at the time were Hungarians, driven out like him by the Soviet invasion of 1956, and he was keen to broaden its base. We set the date for Thursday 18th June 1964, but since the non-conformist church wasn't licensed to register marriages, we had a civil ceremony the day before at the Register Office in Brentford. Our witnesses on this, our official wedding day, were my younger brother Jonathan and my mother, probably the only family members present, and the story goes that the registrar, who had a slight squint, caused momentary consternation by apparently looking at Jonathan to ask the question, 'Do you take this woman ...?'

The following day we drove ourselves to Collingham Gardens, a bigger but still modest party of nine: my parents; my elder brother Robin and his wife Mary; my younger brother Jonathan; my sister Caroline and her fiancé, my old school friend David McFetrich (who were our witnesses for this occasion); and of course bride and groom, he in an ordinary lounge suit, she in an off-white, natural wool suit with matching hat, understated but exquisitely tailored by a Finnish friend who was a professional dressmaker. It did duty on special occasions for decades to come. At the short, spoken ceremony, Mr Patkai was more nervous than we were – it was the first marriage service he had ever conducted in English. Back at Warwick Lodge we enjoyed a quiet family meal before venturing out to the veranda at the back of the house for photographs.

We had done well not to plan a reception in the garden, as it rained incessantly all day. Our few photographs show us huddled on the veranda while the photographer under an umbrella, in turns Jonathan or David, operated the camera (itself under a tarpaulin) on a tripod on the lawn. There was no timer mechanism on the camera, so no single photo shows all nine of us. Even in better conditions, the results would scarcely have been good enough for Raili's parents to show to their friends, so we had sensibly booked a session with a local studio just across Richmond Bridge, over which Raili and I sloshed in mid-afternoon.

The wedding group (back row: Jonathan, my father, Robin, Mary; front row: Caroline, bride and groom, my mother) …

…and the photographers

The official portrait, taken on 18th June 1964

It was a happy occasion nonetheless, and we set off in good spirits for our honeymoon on the west coast of Ireland. We were booked in at the Renvyle House Hotel in Connemara, quite an extravagance, but recommended by my family – Jonathan was studying at Trinity College Dublin, and they had fallen in love with Ireland. To compensate for the expense of the hotel we travelled as cheaply as we could. This meant a late night plane to Dublin and an overnight drive across Ireland in a hire car to avoid the expense of accommodation in Dublin.

It's not every memoirist who would wish to describe their wedding night in detail, but I can, since my hands were firmly attached to the steering wheel throughout that long night. It started inauspiciously with our agent unable to get the tiny Fiat 500 into reverse – it kept jumping forwards towards a brick wall – so that when he gave up and handed the key over to me, my margin for error was reduced to a couple of inches. Happily I succeeded in finding the reverse gear, so dismissed him airily, assuming his inability to get the heater working was also a part of his general incompetence. Alas, here I fared no better. Raili and I froze steadily as we put-putted along the empty roads. The only living soul we saw was a shepherd boy, who inconveniently passed by just as Raili was relieving herself by the roadside. Raili pretended to be picking flowers, but was not prepared for him to come back for a second look to check he wasn't seeing things. Ireland was a sleepy place in those days, and it was only after several villages had met us with bleary-eyed incomprehension that we found a town where we could feed the car and ourselves, and get a room for a couple of hours for a sleep and a wash.

We made an inauspicious start at the Renvyle House Hotel too. Raili was too exhausted to come down for dinner on our first evening. Honeymoon couples were pretty easily identified, and I sensed uncomfortably the other guests' assumption that we had had a row on our first wedded day. We trumped them the following morning, however, when we tucked into our breakfast, disgustingly fresh and dishevelled after our early morning swim. From then on it got better. The mountains shimmered blue, the beaches of crushed shells glistened white, and on our last day the sun burnt the top of my feet as I kicked off my shoes to play tennis on the lush grass court, so that I had to drive back to Dublin barefoot. Our homecoming was slightly chaotic. Jonathan, who was driving us home from Heathrow, was pulled over by the police, as he appeared to be carrying a corpse in the back of the car. It was me, head down and feet up, the only comfortable position. Then Raili cut herself opening a tin in our flat and fainted. I held her up, but my swollen feet wouldn't hold me up, so we collapsed in an ungainly heap on one of the camp beds we had set up to do duty while waiting for Raili's furniture to arrive.

It did arrive in due course and was unloaded from a wooden container that the removal company were about to take away for destruction when I stopped them. The wood was just too good to be lost. So I spent evenings and weekends painfully taking it apart and storing the rough but good quality planks for immediate and later use. I tried to do everything myself – including installing an all-night solid fuel burner for the winter, since our flat had no heating – in order to save money. I always felt hard up, despite having an extra job teaching Spanish at an evening class to add to my Foreign Office salary. Raili, whose considerable qualifications as a teacher of Swedish to Finns counted for nothing in England, went to work behind the counter at the Scandinavian Shop in Regent Street. She gained a valuable new qualification there: how to deal in unfamiliar pounds, shillings and pence. We would often find each other on the train going back from Waterloo to our romantically named station of Strawberry Hill, but after a while Raili became less intent on finding me than a sandwich to still her hunger pangs. She was pregnant.

We did a course with the National Childbirth Trust, which had the great merit of bringing me into the picture. Raili had worried that her unfamiliarity with colloquial English would let her down at a crucial moment if she had the baby in hospital, so we elected to have it at home, which in practice meant my parents' home. At that time one out of every three women gave birth at home. Raili spent the last week or so of her pregnancy comfortably in Warwick Lodge, wandering round the garden or sitting indoors listening to the sound of a tennis ball being lobbed back and forth – it was Wimbledon fortnight.

On the morning of 3rd July 1965 we were up early, Raili with what she took to be contractions. I busily applied the massage techniques I had learnt with the NCT, but the urgently summoned midwife was dismissive: 'You're just playing at having a baby!' she scoffed. Indeed, it was nine o'clock in the evening when a baby girl finally appeared after much pushing and shoving. Ready to give up, the doctor had already summoned an ambulance, but when it arrived my beaming father was sent downstairs to dismiss it. 'Congratulations, sir!' said the driver, assuming he was speaking to the father of the new baby and shaking him warmly by the hand, which of course broadened my father's grin still more.

Our little girl spent a miserable first few hours in this world. Rudely ejected from the soft warmth of the womb into the bony arms of her father so that Raili could rest, she yelled. So we surreptitiously gave her back to her mother, which was against the practice of the time. She was suckled and slept. She already had her name of Karin, independently chosen by both Raili and me for its beautiful sound when we emerged from seeing the 1950s Swedish historical film *Karin Månsdotter*. But it was an impossibly grown-up name for such a tiny thing, so for the first few years of her life she was Pupu – Finnish for a little rabbit.

These were blissful days, where the support of my family made it easy for Raili and me. Within a week or so we were out at the cinema, seeing a comedy about the 'Swinging Sixties' London that was all the rage at the time: *The Knack ... and How to Get It*. The film was enjoyable enough, but as we came out into the daylight the sudden realisation that a new being was waiting for us at home was overwhelming.

By the time Karin was born I knew that I was slated to replace Tony Bishop in Moscow in the autumn. A year earlier I had successfully applied for one of the few established positions in Research Department, and on 7th August 1964 I had been appointed Research Assistant Grade 3 in Branch B (Research) of the Foreign Service. I remember nothing of the interview, which must have taken place shortly after our marriage, but I do remember being worried by one of the conditions of service, requiring anyone 'who proposes to marry a person who has not at all times since her birth been a British subject' to notify Personnel Department. I had unwisely told Raili of this, making her worry that she might find herself standing between me and my career. The Foreign Office had indeed questioned me – had she or her family found themselves behind the Soviet lines during the war? If so, the FO would have been concerned that the Russians might somehow have gained a hold over them. Reassured on that point, they had turned to a more delicate question: would Raili make a suitable diplomatic wife? They had asked my boss Eddie Bolland to vet her informally. Thoroughly embarrassed by the request, Eddie had made an arrangement under which I would take Raili to the theatre, meeting him and George Walden at a nearby pub on the way for a casual drink. Raili had known nothing of the subterfuge and had had sufficient poise (or whatever it was that was required of her) for Eddie to be able to report back favourably.

Those hurdles negotiated, we had been told that Raili would have to take out UK citizenship. This was not difficult. Under the British Nationality Act of 1948 citizenship was available on demand to wives of UK citizens. On 25th January 1965 Raili had duly been registered as a UK Citizen, having sworn her oath of allegiance to the Queen and all her heirs (which unfortunately she pronounced 'hairs', the word being outside her vocabulary at the time). Raili was not being asked to become an instant British patriot: there was a compelling practical reason for the requirement. Only as a British citizen could she enjoy consular protection from the UK authorities when we were in Moscow. But Raili was distressed later to discover that in becoming British she had unwittingly forfeited her Finnish citizenship.

Involved as we were with parenthood, Moscow still seemed a distant prospect, so we were brought up with a jerk when at the end of July I was suddenly asked if we would go out to Moscow immediately. Tony Bishop had been expelled, and they wanted his replacement out there as soon as possible. The sequence of events was as follows. On 25th April 1965 the Soviet authorities had arrested Gerald Brooke, an idealistic but naïve British lecturer in his 20s and (like me) a former postgraduate exchange student. They had caught him handing over to a Russian contact some documents on behalf of the NTS (*Narodno-Trudovoi Soyuz*, or People's Labour Union), a Frankfurt-based Russian émigré organisation dedicated to bringing down the Soviet regime. It was an organisation we suspected of being heavily penetrated by the Soviet security organs. The Foreign Office immediately assumed that Brooke had been framed. To complete the scenario of a Western plot the Russians needed to implicate the British Embassy. A mutual friend had advised Brooke to pass his material to Tony Bishop if he were unable to deliver it to the Russian contact. Tony himself didn't know Gerald Brooke, but for the Soviet court this detail provided sufficient evidence of British official involvement in Brooke's activities.

On 25th July 1965 Brooke was duly found guilty. On 29th July, equally predictably, Tony was declared *persona non grata* and had to leave Moscow, a couple of months before the end of his tour. Hence the summons to me. But the Foreign Office graciously agreed that with a four-week-old baby I couldn't be expected to go to Moscow there and then. There was no question of my going without my family – married men without their wives were considered too vulnerable to approaches by seductive KGB agents. But a new member of Soviet Section, David Miller, was more than willing to go out for a couple of months as a stop gap. David had also been on the postgraduate exchange scheme, in Leningrad, and had come back to complete a further degree on Soviet art history at London University. But it was faltering and David needed to earn his living, so he had secured a temporary post in Soviet Section, as I had earlier.

Gerald Brooke's arrest and trial had many repercussions. He himself paid for his gullibility with a five-year prison sentence, out of all proportion to his trivial offence. The Russians soon revealed their hand: they wanted to exchange him for two convicted Soviet spies, in which they were eventually successful. The price of Tony Bishop's unwitting involvement in Brooke's plans was a long exile from Russia that only came to an end when Tony was the British government's principal Russian interpreter and it became too embarrassing for the Soviet authorities to keep him out. The episode was life changing for David Miller too, though in quite another way: he met and swiftly married the nanny of the British Embassy doctor. Raili and I were scarcely affected, though the episode may have prepared us subconsciously for the buffetings that lay ahead. As it was, we sold our flat for £50 less than we had paid for it, exchanged Karin's magnificent coach-built pram, a family heirloom, for a more practical folding model, and prepared to set off for Moscow.

Three

Moscow 1965-1968

We arrived at Moscow's Sheremetyevo airport on 1st October 1965. 'You must be the new interpreter for the Consular Convention negotiations,' said the gentleman in the bow tie as he came forward to greet me. 'Didn't they tell you that in London?' 'No, they didn't,' I replied grumpily, nervously gripping the handles of the carrycot in which our three-month-old daughter was sleeping placidly. 'But you are Tony Bishop's replacement, aren't you?' he continued imperturbably. 'He did the interpreting, and so will you.' All I needed to know, he added, was the Russian for 'the sending state' and 'the receiving state', which he gave me and I instantly forgot. 'Our first session is tomorrow at ten. Don't worry, I'll be there,' he concluded, a comforting smile spreading across his cherubic face.

I discovered later that he was Tom Brimelow, the second in command at the British Embassy, and he had of course not come all the way to the airport for the sake of a lowly Third Secretary, but to meet Adrian Russell, the straw-haired Australian expert sent out by London to conclude the long-running consular negotiations. Adrian had approached me on the plane, when I had equally vigorously denied any knowledge of my new role.

In truth, I did have a vague idea that I would be expected to interpret at the negotiations in Moscow. But I resented being pitched into it the moment we arrived, having forgotten that the Russians still worked a five-and-a-half-day-week. It was Friday afternoon, and I was looking forward to spending the weekend settling in. The intrusion of work on my family life was something quite new to me, a seasoned commuter used to keeping a measurable distance between home and office. I worried about how Raili would manage our first day without me, new as she was to Moscow.

In fact Raili managed very well. The embassy wives (they were all wives in those days) ran an efficient welcoming system. My fellow Kremlinologist Graham Beel, his wife Mary and their two-year-old daughter had all come to the airport to make us feel at home as a family. Raili was soon introduced to the range of facilities available to ease the passage of the newcomer from West to East – the embassy shop, where orders for a special Christmas delivery from the UK were already being taken, the high quality Finnish milk delivered by the overnight train from Helsinki, the Soviet foreign currency *Beriozka* shops that sold a range of Soviet goods unavailable to ordinary Russians – all the comforts that made up the cosy, self-sufficient world of a Western diplomatic mission in Moscow. This was the set up that I had so despised four years earlier when I had looked at it from the vantage point of a postgraduate student roughing it in the real Soviet Union. But foraging in Moscow for myself as a student was one thing; providing for my family was quite another, and I had no qualms about accepting what was offered.

Our flat was in one of those blocks that housed only Westerners. *Sadovo-Samotechnaya 12/24* was its official address – 'Sad Sam' to successive generations of embassy staff and Western journalists. It had been solidly built by German prisoners of war, with wooden parquet floors and high ceilings with cornices. The flats had a touch of style that was totally missing from more modern blocks, notably those on *Kutuzovsky Prospekt* ('Kut'), where many more Westerners lived. We had a large sitting/dining room at one end and, inconveniently, a kitchen at the other, with two bedrooms in between, all connected by a corridor running down the spine of the flat. It was long enough to wheel Karin's pram up and down on those occasions when she needed the rocking motion but it was too cold or awkward to get her and the pram out on to the street. The other thing that soothed her in the flat, oddly enough, was the six-lane ring road right underneath us and the sight of the lorries (mostly) and cars, the gentle hum of their engines muffled by the double windows.

I also enjoyed watching the world go by on this historic ring road – the *Sadovoe Kol'tso*, or Garden Ring – which followed the circuit of the ramparts originally surrounding the centre of Moscow. One morning, not long after our arrival, I noticed two men surrounded by an inadequate safety barrier making a small hole in the middle of the road. Gradually, it deepened and widened, machinery was brought in

Raili and Karin study the view from our sitting room window

and hoardings set up to protect the work. I was witnessing the birth of a massive flyover that would eventually take this section of the ring road over the top of one of the roads that radiated from the Kremlin at the centre.

The work was slow and hampered by the cold once winter set in. Anti-freeze was a rare commodity at that time, so the cooling system in every item of machinery had to be drained at the end of each working day. The alternative was to leave the engines running overnight, a regular practice in provincial coach parks, but thankfully not in the centre of Moscow. Fires would be lit under the machines to get them going in the morning. One got out of hand, and

I found myself ringing the fire brigade in alarm as the flames reached the height of our flat, only some 20 yards away. The firemen arrived commendably quickly, but by then the workers themselves found a way of dousing the flames – I should have had more faith in the Russian workers' ability to cope by themselves with unscheduled and even dangerous situations.

One thing they couldn't get round, however, was The Plan. Work to drive in the piles that would support the new flyover began sluggishly but increased by the day until they were at it non-stop, only for the operation suddenly to fall silent until the sluggish pile-driving started again and the cycle repeated itself. It took me a while to realise that the manic activity always took place in the last few days of the month and the sluggish work in the first couple of weeks of the following month. I was witnessing the race to fulfil the monthly plan.

On the internal side of our block, not visible from our flat, was a courtyard, where mothers and nannies took their children for a breath of not very fresh air – it also served as a car park. Raili often pushed Karin further down the road to a little square with a few trees and benches. The benches here and in other open spaces were always occupied by old people, with and without children, even in the coldest weather. They were escaping, or perhaps being driven from, the tiny space they were allocated in overcrowded communal flats, which afforded little privacy. When they saw Raili approaching they would sometimes throw themselves heroically in front of the pram to stop Karin falling out, not having noticed that she was securely, but loosely strapped in – the buggy we had taken was unknown in Russia, where prams were smaller versions of the carriage pram we had had in England. Once they had recovered from the shock, the old ladies would berate Raili for not dressing Karin sufficiently warmly – this was a scene familiar to all Western mothers – and if Raili didn't understand the words, she quickly understood their import.

Soon Raili did begin to understand the words. She took up Russian at an early stage in our posting, which was no small thing for a Finn. The Russian and Finnish languages are not related, nor has Russian ever been a widely taught subject in Finnish schools. The Russians, not the Germans, had been the wartime enemy of the Finns. But with her Russian classes, and with ballet classes laid on for the diplomatic wives by the Soviet Foreign Ministry, Raili soon found herself drawn into the life of the country. Our flat was quite central, and while I baby-sat of an evening Raili would tramp through the snow to the Bolshoi Theatre to watch an opera or ballet.

Our home life thus got off to a gentle start, without the tensions that we might have expected from being pitched into the citadel of a hostile ideology. We did seem to get more than our fair share of suspicious telephone calls, often nothing more than 'heavy breathing', but we put that down to the fact that our telephone number happened, exceptionally, to be in the public domain in the Soviet Union. In 1963 the Soviet authorities had tried and convicted Colonel Oleg Penkovsky, a Soviet officer who was British agent (a genuine one, not a put-up job). His well-publicised trial revealed that

Moscow, 1965-1968

Domestic life: the author at home with Karin...

... and Raili and Karin under the walls of the Kremlin

to contact his embassy handlers he was to ring the number K4-89-73. He didn't have to say anything, just blow three times into the mouthpiece, which would give an appropriate signal. This was the telephone number of the British Assistant Naval Attaché at the time, and now it was ours.

Having a small child to focus on kept our feet on the ground. A sensible security briefing in London, given to all staff before they went behind the Iron Curtain, also helped. It was introduced with a reading from a visitor's account of his Russian experience. He had been subjected to eavesdropping, provocative visits to his hotel room and tampering with his luggage while he was out. This was standard practice for the Soviet secret police (officially the Committee for State Security, or KGB, to give it its Russian initials) but the account had in fact been written a century earlier and described the activities of the Tsar's secret police. The KGB had merely taken over a long-established Russian practice; we should not make heavy weather of it, we were advised. But we should remember that we were on the KGB's territory and, if we chose to provoke them, they would get their own back.

I ignored this advice only once, when my brother Jonathan was visiting. To show off, I did a manoeuvre in my car which ensured that my KGB 'tail' shot past me, so that I was able to follow him. It was about the only time I ever saw a Russian driver look in his rear view mirror. The incident had no consequences, but I was given a severe ticking off by Raili and Jonathan for making a pointless gesture.

Most importantly, however, we were told to mind our language at home. There was plenty of evidence that our apartments were bugged, which naturally made embassy staff uncomfortable. Some were frightened to open their mouths at all; some enjoyed addressing outrageous remarks to light bulbs and other fittings assumed to conceal microphones; while many of the junior staff took a nonchalant attitude, saying: 'Why should they be interested in me, when I don't know any secrets?' It was explained to us that the KGB hardly expected to be spoon fed state secrets through a microphone in the wall and would suspect a 'provocation' if it appeared that they were; they were interested in people and their weaknesses.

The alarming case of a former clerk to the Naval Attaché, John Vassall, was held up as an example. A lonely homosexual, who in those days couldn't admit his sexuality even to his own colleagues, he had been lured to an assignation and compromised by the KGB in Moscow in the mid-1950s. Threatened with prosecution, he had signed a document promising to collaborate with the Soviet authorities. He was then blackmailed into carrying out his promise after his return to London. As we started our Moscow posting, Vassall was starting an 18-year prison sentence for passing secrets to the Russians from his job in the Admiralty.

Innocent 'pillow talk' after a party – so-and-so seemed to be having an affair with so-and-so's wife, or was drinking heavily, or seemed chronically short of money – could provide leads for the KGB to follow up. Someone's loose talk had probably put them on to Vassall. The message was straightforward: don't gossip.

I settled easily into my work at the embassy after the first flurry of interpreting at the Consular Convention negotiations was over. Embassy routine was quite rigid. Few of us junior members of staff had cars, so we relied for transport on the fleet of embassy Humbers. These low slung saloons were not well suited to the rough, snowed up roads of Moscow, but the embassy had to run British cars for form's sake. They ferried us to and from work four times a day, since we came home for the traditional diplomatic two-hour lunch break. The rhythm of the working week was decreed by the schedule of the diplomatic bag – bags, in fact, about 20 of them each week, in and out, containing everything from confidential diplomatic mail to our private correspondence (to keep it away from prying Soviet eyes) and a ration of parcels. Like the pile drivers outside our flat, we increased our pace at the embassy as bag day approached, only to slacken off again immediately after. Once I had my own car I would stay late at the embassy on Friday evening to pick up our letters and the regular supply of baby clothes sent out at our request by my parents. In the winter, though, weather conditions frequently played havoc with the schedules. Landing aids at Sheremetyevo were primitive; the British European Airways Comet would sometimes sit for days in Stockholm waiting for the weather to clear.

The British Embassy was an imposing neo-classical mansion built at the end of the 19th century by one of the rich merchant class that had emerged from serfdom to contribute to the surging Russian economy. The Kharitonenko family had made their money from the production of sugar beet in the Ukraine. Like other merchants they had built their Moscow mansion in the unfashionable, 'beyond the Moscow river' (*zamoskvorechie*) district, but the Kharitonenko mansion enjoyed a unique location on the embankment directly facing the Kremlin across the river. St Sophia Embankment (*Sofiiskaya Naberezhnaya*), whose name had entranced me when I used to visit the embassy as a student in 1961, had by 1965 been renamed *Naberezhnaya Morisa Toreza* to commemorate the loyal French Communist Party leader Maurice Thorez, who had died in 1964. Despite the best efforts of the Soviet propagandists, however, the French Communist was less well known to Muscovites than the erstwhile Empress of Austria, and I frequently heard the street referred to as *Naberezhnaya Maria Theresa*. The breathtaking view of the Kremlin from the elegant reception rooms on the first floor remained the embassy's chief attraction.

Like the prestigious office I had occupied in London, however, the price we paid for a fine location and elegant representational rooms was a cramped and awkward working area – indeed the Commercial and Cultural Sections of the embassy were housed far away, in the *Kutuzovsky Prospekt* diplomatic complex. The Russian Secretariat, my office, was located in one of the detached wings of the embassy. We shuttled between our wing and the main building in all weathers, trying not to slither on the ice and scatter confidential papers all over the front courtyard, our every journey doubtless logged and filmed by the KGB from their little watch tower in the factory next door.

The quaint title of 'Russian Secretariat' derived from a proposal in 1944 by the then ambassador, Sir Archibald Clark Kerr, to set up a corpus of specialist 'Russian Secretaries' on the lines of the Oriental Secretaries who analysed and reported on internal political developments in a number of Middle East posts. The man behind the proposal, though, was George Bolsover, then a First Secretary at the Embassy, later Director of the School of Slavonic and East European Studies at London University, whom I faced across the interview table more than once in my student days. In concept it had been a far-reaching scheme. By 1945 the Treasury had agreed to fund a staff of 25, to serve not only in Moscow but in other posts likely to be dominated by the Soviet Union. In practice, though, there were never more than five, all based in Moscow. In the early years after the war the Russian Secretariat was staffed by experts drawn from the academic world, including such luminaries as Max Hayward and Harry Willetts (Oxford), Reg Christian (St Andrews) and Richard Freeborn (London), from the Moscow-based Joint Press Reading Service, whose British, American and Canadian staff had translated and analysed the Soviet press during the war, and from the Foreign Office Research Department (FORD), just then getting under way in London.

By the time I arrived in 1965 the Russian Secretariat had become something of a field station for FORD, but it happened that during my first tour I was initially the department's only man in Moscow. My colleagues Graham Beel and Alex Batten were both seconded to

Moscow from the Information Research Department (IRD), which I had unsuccessfully applied to join when searching for a job in 1963. Despite that department's covert propaganda brief – which was to be exposed in 1977, leading to its closure – in Moscow its members did exactly the same work as I did.

Our boss, Joe Dobbs, was a generalist diplomat who had been pulled out of a pleasant post in Rome to fill the Head of Russian Secretariat seat left vacant by Ted Orchard at the end of his tour. With two Moscow tours behind him – in the late 1940s and early 1950s – Joe was as expert as any of us specialists. More than twenty years older than me, he was rather a distant figure, but a man of unfailing kindness, a quality he extended towards the Russians as well, treating them as basically decent people saddled with a lousy system. In his first posting Joe had supervised the publication of *British Ally*, a weekly Russian language newspaper put out by the British government during and immediately after the war when Britain and the Soviet Union were indeed allied. Something of the wartime spirit of co-operation lingered in Joe. The Dobbs family, Joe, his caustic Australian wife Marie and four precocious sons, lived above us in the *Sadovo-Samotechnaya* block. Marie published two light novels about Moscow under the name of Anne Telscombe (as well as a serious conclusion to Jane Austen's unfinished novel *Sanditon*). Her *Miss Bagshot goes to Moscow* neatly encapsulated the 'village' life of foreigners in Moscow in the late 1950s: Embassies and diplomatic living quarters; hotels for Westerners only; puzzled foreign delegations and equally puzzled Soviet officials trying to fit them into class war stereotypes; news-starved Western journalists; and the eccentric English lady traveller who tries unavailingly to break out of the circle and discover the 'real Russia', only to be foiled by the ever-vigilant Soviet security organs.

While we were in Moscow Marie made no secret of the fact that she was working on another novel. It would feature the KGB man supposedly in the basement of our block monitoring our conversations through the hidden microphones. In her story he would become embroiled in the lives of the diplomats and journalists occupying the flats above him. There's little doubt that there was such a man, more likely a team of them, though they would not have enjoyed the freedom of manoeuvre Marie was bound to give them to make her story work. The idea was a good one, though, and many years later, in 2006, a similar idea inspired the brilliant German film *The Lives of Others*. Asked how she kept her manuscript away from the prying eyes of the KGB, Marie would answer breezily: 'I keep it under the bed. The maid never gets as far as cleaning there!' When *The Listener* was published in 1968 we could tease out some familiar individuals from our block, lightly disguised in the composite characters Marie had created.

Although physically set apart, the Russian Secretariat was an integral part of the political section of the embassy; we were regulars at the morning meeting when we reported on the day's press and took our orders from the ambassador. Sir Geoffrey Harrison was of the old school, tall and patrician, used to things being done at his bidding. He was driven around in a Rolls Royce, at that time standard issue for an ambassador of his status, but a dubious asset in Moscow conditions, although oddly enough a perk enjoyed by Soviet leaders. Lenin had had one, which remained on display in the museum that had been his country house; and so did the current leader Leonid Brezhnev, though it was not seen on the Moscow streets. The ambassador's Rolls suffered from chronic brake failure; he was incensed when told at a morning meeting that once again he would have to make his calls for the day in an ordinary Humber. 'Oh, can't you get that Rolls to the front door, John?' he wailed at his private secretary. 'I can certainly get it to the front door, sir, but I can't guarantee that it will stop once it gets there!' replied the cheeky John Kerr, to suppressed laughter from the rest of us.

I was always a bit scared of the ambassador and was glad that John's barbed remark did him no harm – he went on to become Head of the Diplomatic Service. Although Sir Geoffrey had done an earlier tour in Moscow he displayed no particular interest in Russia, which made Joe Dobbs fret: 'I must get the ambassador out to the theatre some time'. This was Sir Geoffrey's last posting before retirement, and he was 'demob happy'. Only he wasn't happy and became increasingly tetchy. Some years later it was revealed that he had fallen into a KGB 'honey trap' – seduced by one of his maids, Galina. It was almost ridiculous, since among the matronly ladies who served at the ambassador's dinner table, Galina conspicuously flaunted her charms, leaning over the guests in her low-cut uniform. Amber warnings flashed around her. The background, though, was sad. The Harrisons had a disabled daughter, who could not be brought to Moscow, and Lady Harrison spent a fair amount of time in the UK visiting her and leaving Sir Geoffrey isolated in 'the flat above the shop', as the ambassador's residence effectively was. Lonely ambassadors were as vulnerable a KGB target as lonely clerks.

Another reason for Sir Geoffrey's lack of engagement was simply that his No 2, Tom Brimelow, the man in the bow tie who had greeted me on our arrival, pinched most of his work, as he did any other work that was going, including from the typists. He could easily anticipate when the ambassador would demand an urgent telegram on a subject of moment and delighted in wrong-footing everyone by producing a ready-made draft, typed up by himself, the moment the ambassador opened his mouth on the subject. Tom Brimelow was definitely not old school. The son of a Lancashire cotton yarn salesman, he had worked his way up from a lowly job in the consular service. He knew his Soviet Union – he had run the Moscow embassy's consular department during the war and returned on a further posting soon after – but he was a difficult man, not approachable.

Brimelow also poached the political work of the Head of Chancery, Anthony Williams. Anthony was definitely old school, my old school in fact, Oundle, the only diplomat from the school I ever met. Relaxed to the point of apparent nonchalance, he would note down the ambassador's rapid-fire instructions on a corner of his packet of cigarettes, turning it over and over as each free space filled up, his lanky frame flopping ever further into his seat, often with one leg ending up over the arm rest. With no previous Moscow experience, Anthony knew better than to fight Tom Brimelow for turf and focused on the other side of his work, administration. I was astonished when he turned up once in my office to discuss my request for a bigger flat. But distributing the limited range of flats among members of the staff, whose rank and size of family rarely made a neat match, was tricky and important in an embassy where maintaining staff morale in what was for many a hostile environment was a priority.

Once a week Rodric Braithwaite, First Secretary Commercial and a future ambassador, came over from his section's distant office to report to the morning meeting on the latest developments in the economic reform being pursued by the post-Khrushchev leadership. It was known as the Kosygin reform, since the Soviet prime minister was politically responsible for it, or the Liberman reform, its chief theoretician. Put simply, the reform was designed to introduce a bottom-up market mechanism into the top-down command economy, without upsetting the Communist Party's overall economic and political monopoly. As such, it was doomed from the start, but in 1965 it was only just getting under way, and every one took it seriously. Rodric's pithy reports were a delight, as were those of his equally talented successor Julian Bullard, who in the critical year of 1971 was to head the FCO department dealing with the Soviet Union. The embassy was indeed awash with talent: John Kerr had been preceded as the ambassador's private secretary by Andrew

Wood and Brian Fall, both of whom would be my ambassadors three decades later.

They worked in Chancery, the external political section of the embassy, which concentrated on representing British interests in the Soviet Union. Much of their day-to-day work was similar to what we did in the Russian Secretariat – reading, analysing and reporting – but it was conducted at a much faster pace and involved more contact with the Soviet Ministry of Foreign Affairs. I had a taste of it when I was transferred there for a few weeks in June 1967. Chancery was short-handed when Israel launched what came to be known as the 'Six-Day War', a surprise preventive attack on Egypt and its Arab allies. It was a critical period for everybody, not least the Russians, whose prestige as a weapons supplier to Egypt was engaged and who had to parade their anti-Zionism without committing themselves to doing anything. There were many angry Arab students in Moscow who had to be allowed to let off steam, but the Russians were nervous after a recent demonstration of Chinese students outside the American Embassy over Vietnam had turned into a nasty fight between the students and Russian policemen. As supporters of Israel the British were also a target, and one day we found ourselves penned into the embassy with the ends of our road sealed off by street-watering lorries. The few Arab demonstrators who tried to get past them had to face a barrier of mounted police, more lorries and troops. But a few days later, on a quiet Saturday afternoon when there were no reinforcements outside the embassy, a crowd of well-drilled Russian 'demonstrators' passed by on their way between the American and Israeli Embassies and hung up some banners on our railings. One of them, which read: *Pozor angliiskim posobnikam izrail'skoi aggressii! (Shame on the English accomplices of Israeli aggression!)* found its way down to the embassy dacha, where it graced the wall of the loo for many years.

In the Russian Secretariat, by contrast, we had to make our own pace, as the Soviet internal political scene was generally quiet – indeed the Soviet leadership would rather smugly take credit for abandoning the volatility of the Khrushchev years. We tried hard to extend our range beyond reading and reporting the press. Every week we would send a *Miscellany* to London, a light-hearted report that we tried to fill with items not to be found in the press. We attended a regular series of public lectures on international affairs. Here, after sitting patiently through the speaker's standard presentation, we would listen intently as he responded to questions passed up on slips of paper from the floor – some quite barbed – and thus absorb something of the mood of the public.

My brief also included following the cultural scene. It had nothing of the vibrancy of the Khrushchev years, but the broad umbrella of the state still allowed political and artistic deviations from the norm. In the theatre, performers could convey political nuances invisible to the censor in the script of the play. The concert hall fare was more varied than appeared from advertised programmes. We were befriended by Volodya Zakharov, administrator of the Moscow Conservatory, a roguish character who tried to impress me as I entered his office for the first time by ostentatiously hiding away what he called the 'banned' book he said he had been reading. Without doubt a collaborator of the KGB, if not an agent, he nonetheless provided us with tickets for unusual and often unadvertised concerts, such as an evening devoted entirely to sacred music, at which half the audience were Orthodox priests in mufti – conspicuous by their long hair and beards.

The film industry was in flux. The huge *Mosfilm* studio patronised both traditional and innovative directors. I recall vividly the day when its director invited the ambassador and some of his staff to a preview of Sergei Bondarchuk's blockbuster, four-part version of *War and Peace*. On our way there we came across the budding director Andrei Tarkovsky setting up a scene for his own epic, *Andrei Rublev*. He was placing the icon painter against the white-washed wall of a church, about to splash it with paint. Tarkovsky himself was clearly seized with the intensity of the moment, but all he said to us, simply, was: 'I hope the public will like it.'

The public didn't have a chance to judge until five years later, when a cut version was finally released in a Moscow suburb so that the authorities could not be accused of suppressing it. It is only fair to add, though, that *Andrei Rublev* was far too innovative and difficult to be a box office success in Moscow. The majority of Moscow cinemagoers were looking for entertainment that would lift them out of the drudgery of everyday life. The most popular film showing when we arrived in 1965 was *Carry on Nurse*.

The most far-reaching cultural/political event was in fact taking place off stage as far as I was concerned. Shortly after our arrival in October 1965 I was rung up by *The Daily Telegraph's* Moscow correspondent John Miller, whom I had known as one of the Reuters correspondents during my student year in Moscow. He wanted my comment on the recent arrest of two writers, Andrei Sinyavsky and Yulii Daniel, for having smuggled to the West their bitterly satirical novels about the Soviet Union. I had to confess that I had never heard of them, but they were household names by February 1966 when, amid strident regime-generated publicity, they were sentenced to seven- and five-year prison terms respectively for 'anti-Soviet agitation and propaganda'. Although nobody knew it at the time, the Soviet authorities had made a big mistake in reviving the 'show trial' atmosphere of Stalin's days. The intelligentsia were no longer so easily cowed. The defendants' wives had smuggled out a transcript of the trial that was later published by the journalist Alexander Ginsburg as *The White Book*. He himself was then arrested and tried in 1968, provoking more protest, inside as well as outside the Soviet Union. The flame of the 'dissident' movement had been lit and was not to be quenched. Western governments started looking for ways to champion human rights in the Soviet Union that could not be dismissed by the Russians as interference in Soviet internal affairs. Their efforts finally came to fruition in a trade-off with Soviet security concerns in the Helsinki Agreement of 1975. In my time, however, we embassy people observed the principle of 'non-interference' and kept well clear of the Moscow court rooms. Instead we sought out the Western journalists in Moscow, who allowed themselves more freedom to operate at the edge of the Soviet authorities' level of tolerance.

I was fortunate in having one job in my portfolio that could not be done in London. I was the embassy book-buyer. The appetite of Whitehall's Russia-watchers extended to every publicly available source of information, including books. These could only be found in the Moscow bookshops, and it was my job to buy them and ship them back to London through the diplomatic bag. I had three principal customers: my own Research Department, anxious to have reference books or any official government or party records; the Ministry of Defence, which had a broad range of interests, from Russia's geology, geography and natural resources to books on the economy, industry and science; and the mysterious 'Mr Barnes', who had an inexhaustible appetite for dictionaries and books on communications technology. Nobody told me who 'Mr Barnes' was, but it was easy enough for me to guess.

The job fitted me well. I knew the terrain, having spent many hours in Moscow's bookshops as a student. I also knew how to get some sort of service in the notoriously hostile atmosphere of a Moscow shop. I had to abandon my natural inclination to wait to be served and rudely bark *devushka!* (*girl!* – whatever her age) to engage the attention of one of the surly staff behind the counter (there were no open shelves at that time in Moscow shops). The problem lay in retaining her attention against competition from other customers as I stumbled through the obscure titles of the specialised books I had been asked to seek out. So I devised a method of pasting London's requests (culled from a catalogue I would send them) on to cards. Having secured one assistant's momentary attention I put the cards on the counter in front of her and retired patiently to await results. It was an efficient method, as it allowed the girls to see at a glance what I wanted, fetch the book from the shelf or return the card to the pile if it wasn't there, often at the same time as dealing with other customers. Before long I would be staggering out of the shop with a load of books under my arm. Once they got to know me as a regular customer, the girls behind the counter thawed out. I knew that in part their surliness derived from a fear of being equated with the fawning shop assistants that they understood were the norm in 'bourgeois' countries – they confused service with servility. But although they lacked sales technique, like every Soviet organisation they had a Plan to fulfil. The clever girls in the Academy of Sciences bookshop knew perfectly well that I was not buying for myself and used me to off-load titles that were proving difficult to shift. 'Since you're buying a book on volcanoes,' they might say, 'you will surely be interested in this *Survey of Phreatomagmatic Eruptions*' and hand me a dusty volume that had lain on the shelf for years, knowing that I couldn't possibly reveal my ignorance of the subject. I must have been fed some valuable stuff as well, since before long the embassy received a letter from my clients in London commending my diligence and skill not only in meeting their requirements but occasionally anticipating them.

I worked in close harness with my American colleagues; we would tip each other off when an interesting book appeared on the shelves. I was almost always the beneficiary. After all, there were four of them, full-time Publications Purchasing Officers and not part-time book-buyers like me. They would go on provincial tours equipped with collapsible cardboard boxes, which they would fill with their purchases of locally published books, unavailable in Moscow, to be air freighted back to the embassy. I had one little triumph, however. One Sunday afternoon we were out for a family walk not far from our flat when we passed a kiosk selling general stationery items. Instinctively I ran my eye over the few books stacked up at the back of the kiosk and to my amazement spotted a telephone directory. Domestic telephone directories were non-existent, but very occasionally a directory of public institutions would appear. This was gold dust to the Western intelligence community, as it allowed them to match the names, addresses and telephone numbers of official bodies, including some in the less accessible areas of science and defence on which they would probably have only fragmentary information. Hands trembling with excitement, I bought my copy and asked the assistant if she had any more. 'About twenty,' she replied indifferently. Abandoning my family, I rushed home to fetch my car – it was either that or turning Karin out of her pram to accommodate the booty – and bought the entire stock. The next day I was for once able to tip off my American colleagues and generously reserve for them one of my haul in case they arrived too late at the shops.

Book buying became easier and more fun once I had my own car and was able to make short raids on the shops whenever I wanted, dispensing with the tedious process of booking an embassy vehicle. The car transformed our domestic life as well. We were now able to get out to the Moscow suburbs – strictly within the 40-kilometre radius to which foreigners were restricted – and particularly to our favourite oasis of *Serebryany Bor*. This 'silver pine forest', almost entirely surrounded by water, concealed many old dachas, small but elegant wooden houses set among the pine trees, including the British Embassy dacha, which one could book for a weekend. The forest retreat breathed 'old Russia' and was a haven of peace and quiet. The long journey by tram and bus had been daunting for us, with a pram to carry, but it was only half an hour away by car.

As a junior member of staff I wasn't expected to do representational duties, so I didn't have to run a British car. Like many of my colleagues I bought a *Moskvich* – the only decent small family saloon the country produced. For most Soviet citizens a *Moskvich* was no more than a dream. Only those whose turn in the queue had finally come after a wait of many years could own one, unless they had connections which allowed them to jump the queue or had acquired hard currency during stints working abroad. Soviet-made items of any value could be acquired instantly for hard currency, and with four or five hundred US dollars in our pocket we Western diplomats could just walk into the sales compound and drive out in a new car. But we had to take care to buy the right one – the No. 2 at the Australian Embassy had been lucky to get away without injury when the engine of his new *Moskvich* blew up as he was leaving the compound.

I went off one cold winter's day with the Military Attaché's Russian driver as my guide and the advice from the other embassy drivers ringing in my ears: look at the date of manufacture in order to avoid anything built towards the end of the month, when cars will have been thrown together ever more frantically to fulfil the month's Plan. It was a slow business, as the cars were standing deep in snow, with their cooling systems drained for lack of anti-freeze. So they had to be cleared of snow, thawed out and filled with water. Some of them just didn't respond to this treatment, so we moved down the line one by one. Eventually we found one which started and warmed up satisfactorily. But just as we were about to drive it off, the interior filled up with scalding steam and we had to make a quick exit. A poorly connected pipe somewhere, muttered the salesman, and we moved on once again.

The bright red car that we eventually chose proved sturdy and on the whole reliable. It responded to rough treatment, as one of the embassy drivers demonstrated when I complained that I couldn't get it into gear – the problem was nothing more than my delicate English touch. We had anti-freeze, so were able to keep the car outside in all temperatures. I could usually get it to start, even at minus 20°C, if I woke it up with a kettle of hot water splashed over the engine and some vigorous turns of the crank handle.

Driving in Moscow in those days was easy, and when my reverse gear really did fail, I drove happily around for a week without using it – by that time I knew my routes well enough to ensure that I never stopped in a place that I couldn't get out of in a forward gear. Spare parts were scarce, and when someone broke a quarter light to steal the car radio I had to abandon my original effort to replace it from a local spare parts depot far out of town in favour of ordering it from the shop of last resort – Stockmann in Helsinki. I was careful never to leave the windscreen wipers on the car – they were easy prey for thieves. On the few occasions when I was invited to a Western embassy's National Day reception I caused amusement to the crowd of idle Russians that always gathered in the street to ogle the Western cars rolling up. Stepping out of my modest *Moskvich* I would carefully put the windscreen wipers in my pocket.

While the car could trundle us around Moscow, to get further afield I would have to arrange an official trip, a time consuming and frustrating process. Lack of information made it hard even for Russians to travel in their own country. Links between Moscow and the provinces were well known, but the extensive network between provincial cities much less so. You had to examine the diagram of local links that was displayed in every regional airport to get the picture. The enterprising Director of the Scott Polar Institute in Cambridge, Dr Terence Armstrong (1920-1996), would note these down during his travels to the Soviet North and eventually published a comprehensive diagram of Siberia's air links in the institute's journal, for which he was warmly thanked by his Soviet academic colleagues. They realised that they had wasted many hours flying to

Moscow and out again to reach cities that were in fact linked laterally.

Travellers from the embassy faced constraints even when flying in a straight line from Moscow to the provinces. The Soviet Union was dotted with areas that were closed to foreigners, and if one's route to an open city involved a refuelling stop in a closed one, the Ministry of Foreign Affairs, whom we had to notify before travelling, refused to 'register' the journey. Things were made even more difficult by unpredictable closures of open regions when military exercises were taking place in the area. Our own Army, Navy and Air Attachés not only travelled ceaselessly, but filed daily travel notifications simply to get an idea of where exercises were taking place. Furthermore, embassy security rules required us to travel in pairs, so for each journey I had to find a companion who could spare the time. No wonder the ambitious travel plans we set ourselves were consistently under-fulfilled.

We in the Russian Secretariat faced a further complication. In parallel with registering the trip we would try to arrange talks with local officials. We found this fairly easy when visiting one or other of the 14 Union Republics that together with the Russian Federation (today's Russia) made up the Soviet Union. These Union Republics were nominally sovereign (and today are all independent countries) so they boasted Ministries of Foreign Affairs. I recall being well received in Kazakhstan, Uzbekistan and Kirghizia in 1967 – they quite welcomed the attention we gave them. Ordinary provincial centres in the Russian Federation were harder, as they lacked officials whose job it was to deal with foreigners, and most of them didn't really want to be bothered, knowing that we were seeking information and had nothing to offer them in return.

In between the Union Republics and the ordinary regions came the so-called Autonomous Republics of the Russian Federation, official homelands of some of its many national minorities. My first outing was to Ufa in the foothills of the Urals, over 1,000 kilometres (600 miles) east of Moscow. Ufa was the capital of the Bashkir Republic, homeland of the Turkic Bashkirs, and had for centuries been the spiritual centre of Islam in Russia. Although the Soviet regime itself preached atheism, it tolerated religious orders that did not proselytise and whose leaders could be relied upon to defend Soviet 'freedom of religion' in international forums. Islam was one of these. We were welcomed by the Chief Mufti, with whom we had a stilted conversation, but otherwise the local authorities left us to our own devices apart from attaching a man to follow us. We lost him by accident when we jumped into a taxi on a whim, looking for the local ethnographic museum. Our big surprise, however, was to bump into a large crowd of resident British engineers engaged in constructing a gas plant near Ufa. They assumed we had come out specially to see how they were getting on and entertained us to fried eggs and Soviet champagne in their lodgings. My travelling companions Brian Fall and Andrew Wood, being agile diplomats, managed to show an informed interest in the engineers' life and work, while successfully concealing the fact that we had been completely ignorant of their presence. So we returned to Moscow with a list of their requests and a grumble at the embassy's Commercial Section for not telling us about this British community in the heart of Russia.

The episode in Ufa demonstrated that Westerners with something to offer could penetrate parts of the Soviet Union that political tourists like me found hard to reach. I was fortunate to be chosen by our Cultural Attaché John Morgan (who later served as ambassador to Poland and Mexico) as his travelling companion on trips where he had business to do and was therefore made welcome. I recall going with him to Kishinev, capital of the then Soviet Republic of Moldavia, to visit a postgraduate student, and as far as Ulan Ude, capital of the Buryat Republic, beyond Lake Baikal and just on the Soviet side of the Mongolian border. We were paving the way for a young Cambridge anthropologist, Caroline Humphrey (now Professor Caroline Humphrey DBE), who was to come out to research her PhD thesis on the Buryat people, the first stage of a distinguished academic career. The area had only recently been declared open to foreigners, and as the first Westerners to visit we were received more than hospitably. Ulan Ude itself had long been an important Russian trading post and despite being further east than Singapore looked a very Russian city – an outpost of empire. But outside Ulan Ude was the country's principal Buddhist monastery – Buddhism being another tolerated religion. It was on a freezing plain, where the wind kept the prayer wheels spinning but a sacred baobab tree just survived in a heated mini-greenhouse. On learning that John Morgan had experience of China and Mongolia, the monks

The USSR in Europe, showing places visited

quizzed him eagerly on the international situation and on their spiritual leader, the exiled Dalai Lama. They rewarded him with a model Buddha, and me with a smaller one, 'because you're only a Third Secretary,' they explained. The trip took its toll; we were treated to a massive meal at a collective farm – mutton washed down with Soviet brandy. Desperately thirsty, I asked for something non-alcoholic to drink and was offered a cup of warm fat.

Despite this and similar trials that attended official trips, travel outside Moscow was always rewarding. Sometimes, when John was free, we just decided to go somewhere, so lined up a list of destinations to be probed. Thus, having failed to get to the southern republics of Kalmykia and Daghestan (open, but the vital jumping off point of Astrakhan was closed), and to Vologda in the heart of Russia (too close to a major camp for political prisoners), we once ended up, interestingly for me, in Petrozavodsk, capital of the Karelian Republic, which bordered on Finland.

For me the most relaxing and satisfying trip of all was the one that took us over that border and out of the Soviet Union altogether – on the overnight train to Helsinki. There was no need to change the bogeys at the border, since in Finland as in Russia the track was broad-gauge, a legacy of Finland's history before independence as a Grand Duchy under the Tsars. In the summer of 1966 we had an idyllic family holiday in the house Raili's parents had bought for retirement but were not yet occupying. My brother Jonathan drove my parents out to meet Raili's for the first time and to sample the

Family group in Finland, 1966. From the left, my brother Jonathan, Raili, me, Karin, Raili's
mother, my father and mother, and Raili's father

particular delights of Finland – picking berries in the forest and enjoying the sauna, which they were so taken with that they had one built in the basement of their Twickenham house.

We returned to Moscow in mid-September 1966 with an addition to our family – Raili's cousin Marjatta, whom Raili had taken under her wing in her teaching days in Hamina. Our social life in Moscow had developed to the point where we needed a regular baby-sitter, and Marjatta was the ideal person. There were plenty of other Finnish nannies in Moscow at the time for company. With Marjatta to accommodate we were assigned a bigger flat in a smaller diplomatic block in *Narodnaya Ulitsa*, near a busy square, *Taganskaya Ploshchad'*, and the popular theatre of the same name. It was a rather less prestigious part of the city (it had been given its deliberately proletarian name, 'People's Street', in 1922), but provided a convenient drive to the embassy with a stunning view of the Kremlin whichever side of the river I drove along. This was the start of Marjatta's long and beneficial association with our family in the most peripatetic period of our life. At home, Marjatta weighted the language balance heavily towards Finnish, so Finnish was not only Karin's mother tongue (from birth Raili had spoken only Finnish to her) but, with her father the lone advocate of English and absent most of her waking hours, her natural language. It didn't take her long to learn, however, that 'Mummy says this and Daddy says that' for the same thing, and in time she became perfectly bilingual.

Part of our more outgoing social life stemmed simply from our getting to know more people. Early in 1966 the sound of music began to echo round our Sad Sam staircase – Peter and Joyce Maxey had arrived, she an accomplished pianist, he an aspiring flautist, so I would join them with my flute on Sunday evenings. They also started a singing group, to which Raili and I both belonged. But much of our busier social calendar wasn't entirely voluntary. Although I had developed an early aversion to diplomatic entertaining, we had an entertainment allowance that we were obliged to use. It was doled out in all posts to encourage those members of the embassy who had diplomatic status to entertain and influence local dignitaries. But it was virtually impossible to get Russians to the dinner table unless they could demonstrate to their authorities that they were being invited to meet a delegation from the

UK. At that stage my job didn't include hosting UK delegations, so like many Western diplomats we spent our allowance entertaining other Western diplomats.

Thanks to Raili's initiative and Finnish connections, however, we did occasionally break away from the repetitive sit-down dinners. She organised a traditional Finnish Shrove Tuesday party in which we sent our guests hurtling down a nearby snow-covered slope on makeshift sledges shouting 'Long flax!' – the longer the slide the longer the stalks of flax at harvest time – before reviving them with mulled wine and pies.

We once shipped two buckets of crayfish in from Helsinki and invited guests who understood the delicacy – some Finns and the few Russians who would brave the 'militiaman' who guarded our entrance. The occasion wrecked my nerves, as the Finns and Russians disagreed fundamentally over one piece of crayfish anatomy. The Finns said it was the choicest morsel, as well as the hardest to tease out of the shell, while the Russians wouldn't touch it, claiming it was poisonous. Happily the Russians were wrong and nobody expired overnight (I rang round the next morning to check). I no longer remember who our intrepid Russian guests were, but as well as the roguish Volodya Zakharov, administrator of the Moscow Conservatory, they were probably drawn from among the English teachers at Moscow University. The Professor of English Ol'ga Sergeevna Akhmanova, a long-standing embassy contact, had a sufficient understanding with her own Soviet authorities to be able to give the staff of her faculty some licence to socialise.

When we came back from our home leave in early 1967 the Russians were gearing themselves up for a major celebration: the 50th anniversary of the Bolshevik Revolution of October 1917. The occasion sorely needed a living figurehead as its focus, but there wasn't one. Although three years had passed since Khrushchev had been overthrown, and Brezhnev was quietly gathering ever more levers of power to himself, the new leadership was still maintaining a collective front. Brezhnev was anyway scarcely a charismatic figure. 'Is there a cult of personality in the Soviet Union?' went the street joke, using the euphemism for Stalin's excesses. The answer was: 'There is a cult, but no personality.' During the celebrations the only personality who could be safely held aloft as unimpeachable was Lenin, and held aloft he was: I nearly crashed my *Moskvich* one evening when, rounding a bend on my way to the embassy, I was startled by an outsize moon face of Lenin looking benignly down at me from the sky. When I recovered my poise I realised that Lenin was emblazoned on a huge banner illuminated by searchlights and held up on helium balloons tethered to the ground.

The year also marked the 50th anniversary of Finnish independence, and it was at the magnificent party thrown by the Finnish Embassy, its entrance illuminated by flaming torches, that I bumped into the new Soviet leader. It was only thanks to Raili of course that we had been favoured with an invitation – by that time she was doing some teaching at the Finnish school. We had felt fairly small among the dignitaries, so had headed for a fairly small cloakroom, where I bumped, bottom to bottom, with a large man who appeared, like me, to be taking off his galoshes. When we both straightened up I recognised him immediately, Leonid Brezhnev, combing back his hair in the inimitable Soviet style, and he clearly thought he ought to recognise me – I had strayed into the VIPs' cloakroom.

Then it was the KGB's turn to celebrate its 50th anniversary. The new Bolshevik regime had lost no time in setting up a security service in December 1917 to 'defend the revolution'. It had developed into a monster that in Stalin's time practically devoured the state itself. A key element of Khrushchev's 'de-Stalinisation' programme had been partially to dismantle its huge network of prison camps and to license a limited discussion of the excesses of the Stalinist era. The new leaders thought that here as elsewhere Khrushchev had gone too far; they used the anniversary to re-paint the KGB in heroic colours – as the 'sword and shield' of the state – passing over in silence its long and brutal history of repression.

The ambassador commissioned me to draft a despatch (a formal communication from an ambassador to the Secretary of State) to mark the occasion, adding, a little unnecessarily, I thought: 'Dip your pen in acid!' I set about my task enthusiastically, perhaps too much so when I bought a ticket for a public lecture on the KGB as part of the series that we regularly attended at the Polytechnic Museum. A week before the event the lecture had mysteriously disappeared from the advertised list, to be replaced by a lecture on the GDR – East Germany. The authorities had clearly had second thoughts about making the KGB lecture a public occasion. I had my ticket in my hand, however, when I boldly went up the stairs to the landing that gave on to two lecture halls, a big one to the left and a small one to the right. The young man at the top ushered me towards the smaller one, indicating that the GDR lecture was the one for me, but I wasn't having any of it. Our polite, but pithy exchange required only four words in Russian:

- [He] *Vam GDR?*
- [Me] *Nyet, KGB!*

And I swept into the large hall. Any thrill I might have derived from sitting among a crowd of Soviet spooks quickly disappeared when I found myself surrounded by middle-aged women who would not have surprised me by taking out their knitting. The KGB headquarters was just up the road in *Lubyanskaya Ploshchad'*, and they were presumably some of its army of clerks and indexers who had been told to go to the lecture on their way home. They didn't pay much attention to the speakers' heavily trimmed history of their organisation and its legal basis.

Nor did I, until the last speaker got on to the subject of the wicked imperialists, still plotting the overthrow of the Soviet Union, when I began to have qualms. They soon turned to fear that suddenly a spotlight would be trained on me and the speaker would dramatically declare: 'And there's one among you now!' All eyes would turn on me while I squirmed in my seat. Fear turned to panic and I made for the exit, closely followed by my own personal KGB 'tail'.

He had been with me since the summer. The KGB tended to put a tail on Western diplomats from about six months before the end of their tour. I never knew why, but I suppose the calculation was that if a diplomat was in fact running agents, this would be the time he would have to contact them to make handover arrangements, so would be more likely to give himself away. Small and splayfooted, my man padded around after me or followed in an inconspicuous car and doubtless wrote a detailed report about what the 'object' (he wouldn't have known my name) had done that day. Around this time he would have noted that I saw several of the films put out to romanticise the KGB in its 50th year. I can remember nothing of their content, but in Leningrad they were having a profound effect on the 17-year-old Vladimir Putin. In a frank autobiographical series of interviews published in 2000, when he first became president, Putin said he had wanted to become a pilot, but 'books and films like *The Sword and the Shield* won me over'. Something of a loner, Putin revealed that what had struck him most was how one intelligence officer could do more than whole armies in deciding the fate of thousands of people.

All countries find it difficult to reconcile the need to keep their intelligence operations secret with the desire to boost morale and justify the expenditure of public money by publicising their successes. The Soviet Union had even more inhibitions than most – an obsession with secrecy and a 'holier than thou' attitude which implied that only the 'imperialists' needed to resort to subversion of the other side. So the Soviet Union's major intelligence coups abroad had received virtually no publicity before 1967. In the UK these had included the recruitment in the 1930s of three young men from Cambridge University who later joined the British Foreign Office and Secret Intelligence Service – Donald Maclean, Guy Burgess and Kim Philby. Burgess and Maclean had fled to Moscow in 1951 and Philby in 1963. In 1966 they were joined by another British intelligence officer, George Blake. He had been tried and sentenced in 1961 but had been 'sprung' in 1966 from Wandsworth Prison by a group of sympathisers, among them an Irish petty criminal, Sean Bourke, who ended up in Moscow with Blake. Blake was still invisible while we were in Moscow, but I remember Sean Bourke turning up at the front desk in the embassy one evening just as we were leaving work. He said that he was fed up with Russia and wanted to go home. This raised a brief kerfuffle – should we arrest him on the spot or give him political asylum, thus scoring a propaganda victory? Happily for us, Bourke was an Irish citizen, so this hot potato wasn't for us to handle.

Burgess had died in 1963; Maclean was living a more or less normal life, writing articles on foreign affairs in a Soviet journal; and in 1967 the Russians cautiously allowed Philby to come into the public eye. He gave an interview to the government newspaper *Izvestiya* and turned up in person at the theatre on 12th December for a performance of *All's Well that Ends Well*, given by the visiting Royal Shakespeare Company. Half the British Embassy were there of course, including Raili and me, and from our gallery seat we could see Philby with Melinda Maclean (who had temporarily abandoned her husband) in the stalls below. At the end of the interval Philby came back to his seat first, but couldn't sit still. A bundle of nerves, he kept standing up and looking around for Melinda to return and only subsided when she did, just before the curtain went up. For all his later protestations that he felt at home in the Soviet Union I don't think the play's title applied to him.

The fact that three British officials had been 'turned' by the KGB and were living in Moscow was of course humiliating for the British Government and embarrassing for the embassy. No word of this got into the ambassador's despatch (and I can no longer discern how much of my original draft survived its upward journey) but the final version came to an important conclusion. This was that to evade responsibility for its own repressive role in Soviet society the KGB had an interest in shifting the blame on to 'imperialist subversion'. As a result, the KGB would work against any improvement in bilateral relations with the UK and would override efforts in this direction by other arms of the Soviet government. This proved to be the case despite the best efforts of Labour Prime Minister Harold Wilson. He visited Moscow no fewer than three times during my tour, with interesting results for me.

Four

Getting across to the Russians

O n 15th October 1964 a general election in Britain had returned the Labour Party to power after 13 years in opposition. Harold Wilson became the new prime minister. On the same day the Soviet Union also acquired a new prime minister, Aleksei Kosygin, who together with the new Communist Party leader, Leonid Brezhnev, took the place of the ousted Nikita Khrushchev. British ministers flocked to Moscow in increasing numbers: Wilson (the driving force) came out to Moscow three times during my posting; George Brown as foreign secretary twice; and Michael Stewart, who both preceded and succeeded Brown, once.

I was not involved in the substance of these high-level exchanges. I was a junior member of the embassy focusing on Soviet internal developments rather than Soviet relations with the UK. But as one of the embassy's better Russian-speakers I was called on as a general factotum and occasional interpreter. Indeed, starting on my first working day at the embassy, I had been interpreting at the final round of the negotiations for the Consular Convention, which Michael Stewart signed on 2nd December 1965. My job on that occasion was to seize the precious document as soon as it had been signed and bear it safely back to the embassy. There was a worry that it might otherwise be mislaid while the two foreign ministers and their parties enjoyed a convivial lunch at the elegant mansion that the Ministry of Foreign Affairs used for ceremonial events. I had had a more substantial job before that, sitting for hours with the Soviet interpreter Vladimir Faékov meticulously proof-reading the agreed Russian and English texts. I enjoyed this work. Only four years earlier I had been a student in Moscow; co-operating with Russians, especially those my age, still came more naturally than confronting them, as Cold War attitudes seemed to require. I got to know Vladimir well enough to ask him about his surname. Could it be Turkic? My erudition had blinded me to a simpler explanation. It was a Russian name, albeit not a common one, to which he had added the 'e' to save embarrassment among the English-speaking officials with whom he worked.

Exchanges during the negotiations themselves had been polite. This was a technical agreement setting out procedures for each country in its dealings with nationals of the other country on its territory. But political and security issues lurked beneath the surface – both between the two countries and within them. With the Russians being capricious about permitting consular visits to Gerald Brooke, who by then was serving the first year of his sentence in a Moscow prison, we wanted the Convention to guarantee regular access by consuls to their nationals in detention. The Russians responded by trying to stretch the concept to allow their representatives access to Soviet political refugees in the UK, including those who didn't actually want to see them. This worried the Home Office, while the Security Service had another worry. The FCO wanted a provision in the Convention that would allow us to open a consulate in Leningrad and extend our 'reach' within the Soviet Union. But this would mean allowing the Russians to open a Soviet consulate in Edinburgh. And that would stretch MI5's surveillance resources to the limit. We suspected that on the Soviet side there were tensions between the KGB and the Ministry of Foreign Affairs. When the KGB had somebody in its clutches it was not used to being constrained by the legal procedures of its own government, still less by some agreement with a foreign power. The Russians were already making clear that they were holding Brooke hostage for two of their spies, Peter and Helen Kroger, serving sentences in the UK. Making difficulties over consular access to Brooke and visits from his wife were just aspects of the blackmail they were to exercise ever more blatantly over the next few years. As the ambassador was to note in his despatch on the KGB two years later, the intransigence and cynicism shown in the treatment of Gerald Brooke was inconsistent with the generally more constructive approach of the Soviet Government to bilateral relations with the UK.

The unpropitious background did nothing to deter Harold Wilson, who couldn't wait to get to Moscow. He reckoned that he understood the Soviet system and could establish a 'man-to-man' rapport with the Soviet leaders. He had some reason to think so. By the time he became prime minister, Wilson had no fewer than 13 visits to Moscow behind him. In 1947, as Secretary of Overseas Trade in the post-war Labour government, he had striven unsuccessfully for an agreement to exchange British engineering products for Soviet grain, negotiating into the small hours with the Soviet vice-premier Anastas Mikoyan. In opposition in the 1950s he paid several more visits to the Soviet Union, acting as adviser to a timber importing firm; and as leader of the opposition in the early 1960s he met Khrushchev twice. In his eagerness to get to Moscow he overrode Foreign Office reservations – it was actually London's turn to host a prime ministerial visit – and set off in January 1966 with a large delegation. It included two ministers, Lord Chalfont (disarmament) and Frank Cousins (technology), his Chief Scientific Adviser, Sir Solly Zuckerman, and his wife Mary.

For reasons of security the prime minister's plane was not to spend any time on the ground in Moscow unattended by its crew – it would be too tempting a target for KGB tampering. So immediately after disgorging the incoming party, the plane would take off again for London loaded with diplomatic bags and members of the embassy who wanted a couple of days in London and could be spared – primarily families of staff. Anxious to show off our six-month-old daughter to her English grandparents, we impulsively booked seats for Raili and Karin. But as the day approached the weather closed in, with snow and thaw alternating. Flights were delayed and, worst of all, a Soviet *Tupolev* airliner crashed on take-off from Moscow because of the slush on the runway. Why risk it? With a flurry of apologetic telegrams to my parents, we cried off.

We did well. On 21st February a large number of greeters, Russian and British, were assembled at the Soviet VIP airport of Vnukovo, south of Moscow, watching expectantly as Wilson's plane appeared out of the gloom, only to see it veer away at the last minute. The pilot had decided to head for Sheremetyevo, the international airport to the north of Moscow, where landing facilities were a little better. There followed a mad chase of limousines (and the busload of embassy families) across Moscow, with Soviet prime minister Kosygin and assorted other Russian dignitaries shooting out on to the tarmac from different doors in the Sheremetyevo terminal just in time to greet Wilson as he stepped off the plane.

The process was repeated at the end of the visit, with the plane again being diverted to Sheremetyevo and another Monte Carlo rally round the outskirts of Moscow along the new ring road. The embassy families got home towards midnight instead of the scheduled early evening. I was relieved that mine was not among them.

I was in any case quite nervous as I had been assigned the role of aide-de-camp to Mary Wilson. In the event my anxieties were groundless, as she was a joy to work with. Unassuming and loyal to her husband, she was still her own person and not afraid to admit that she hated being the prime minister's wife. Her happiest time was when Harold was a don at Oxford, she told me, and she shuddered at the thought that the moment they returned to London they would have to go off to the Durham Miners' Gala.

A joy to work with: the Prime Minister's wife Mary

Thanks to being at hand for Mary Wilson I had a ringside seat at the embassy dinners as a 'non-eating interpreter'. Wilson was in his element, never letting the company forget that this was his 14th visit and how pleased he was to see his old friend Anastas, who had been in at the start. Mikoyan, the great survivor from the Stalin era, was indeed still there and gave a weary smile in response. Neither he nor

Mary, sitting next to him, enjoyed small talk, but conversation had to be made, so Mikoyan turned and asked her a standard question: did she have children? Mary gave an audible sigh and trotted out the reply she must have used hundreds of times about their sons. Realising that there was no progress to be made on this front, Mikoyan mischievously remarked: 'You know, the British put me in prison in 1918!' Completely floored by this revelation of her country's wickedness, Mary had to make a very British apology: 'Oh, I'm so sorry!' Mikoyan had indeed been one of the 26 Baku commissars imprisoned when in the maelstrom of the Russian revolution the Soviets were briefly ousted from Baku, capital of the Caucasian republic of Azerbaijan, and British troops occupied the city. But Mikoyan was not going for the kill. Having succeeded in discomforting his guest he laughed it off: 'That was a long time ago!'

There were other people round the table who couldn't understand each other without my help and not very well with it. Frank Cousins, very proud of being Minister of Technology, asked Mrs Polyansky if her husband, Deputy Prime Minister Dmitri Polyansky, was also a minister. 'No, he's higher than that,' replied Mrs P. '*Can* you be higher than a minister?' the deflated Cousins asked me in a whisper. But on learning that Polyansky dealt with agriculture, Cousins was back on the attack: 'I own a farm,' he boasted. Now it was Mrs P's turn to be flummoxed. She had doubtless been briefed that Frank Cousins, a leading trades unionist, was a doughty defender of the rights of the labouring masses, and here he was presenting himself as a full-blown capitalist landowner. 'Is he labour or conservative?' she whispered to me urgently.

After the meal the party split up. In the ambassador's most elegant drawing room facing the Kremlin I joined the ladies' group for coffee, Mrs Wilson, Lady Harrison, Mrs Kosygin and Mrs Gromyko, wife of the Soviet foreign minister, two comfortable Russian matrons. The smallest of small talk followed: whether their husbands favoured tea or coffee when they came in tired from work. 'How I love to talk about everyday things!' gushed Mrs K at one point. But there was a limit even for her, and when everyone fell silent Lady Harrison turned to me and asked after our daughter, whom she had met a month or so previously on a pastoral visit to some embassy flats. 'Can she sit up yet?' Full of pride and enthusiasm I assured Lady Harrison that she could, and was just about to tell the assembled company how she not only sat, but sat *on her potty* without support ... when happily a warning light came on in my brain.

Eventually, with Wilson and Kosygin looking set to go on talking late into the night, the ladies were allowed to go their separate ways. Now without employment, but curious, I wandered into the neighbouring room and hung around on the edge of the circle of advisers behind Wilson, who was trying to convince Kosygin that Britain's policy on the war in Vietnam was not identical to the Americans' and that Britain had an independent role to play in any peace settlement alongside the Soviet Union. Both countries had the necessary status as co-chairmen of the 1954 Geneva Conference on

Southeast Asia. Wilson quoted a statement that underlined our independence from the United States. 'A government statement?' asked Kosygin, probingly. No, Wilson acknowledged, but it was in the Labour Party's election programme. And here he tossed his head backwards towards his circle of advisers, indicating, 'Get it!' Everyone pretended to be busy looking, but they knew there wasn't a copy in the embassy: party political documents were not our business. Kosygin came to our rescue, remarking acidly: 'I'm not interested in party documents, but in government statements.'

Later, Kosygin suddenly produced a document of his own, like a rabbit out of a hat, in Russian only. I think it was a draft Treaty of Friendship. Once again Wilson tossed back his head, and this time the document too, which landed with Howard Smith, Head of Northern Department. 'Translation' he said, curtly, and tossed it to Peter Maxey, who in turn tossed it, like a rugby ball going out to the wing, to me. I was no wing three-quarter and idly locked it away in my office safe. It was late, I wanted to go home, and I would do it first thing the next morning. At that point the warning light came on again: it might be a good idea to check when the translation was wanted. 'Within the hour,' came the terse answer from Howard Smith. It was past midnight by now, and I wondered how I would get it typed up. One of the PM's staff led me down to the ambassador's office, now taken over by the PM, where a couple of typists were dozing over their machines, waiting for just this sort of job. I dictated a translation straight on to the page, gave it to Peter Maxey and went home, my bacon saved.

I was completely new to the 24-hour day worked by prime ministers and their staff. The following morning when I came in to the Embassy to join Mrs Wilson's day of sight-seeing – schools, ballet classes and so on – I was astonished to see Tom Brimelow and John Morgan coming out, ashen-faced. They had been working all night on the prime minister's television address to the Soviet people. Every head of state or government on an official visit was given a five-minute slot at the end of the main news. Against the backdrop of his national flag, the dignitary, head down, would read out a monotonous list of his country's achievements, a Russian voice-over interpretation making it comprehensible to the public – in theory millions-strong, in practice probably a few dozen who had a special interest in the country concerned. Harold Wilson, who was determined to get himself across to the Russian people, was going to do it differently. He had brought with him a rudimentary teleprompter, with its own engineer, Mr Garrett. He had used it successfully on television in the UK. With its help he would be able to deliver his message straight to camera and so face the Russian people eyeball to eyeball. Once in Moscow he and his party were seized by hubris. He would do one better and deliver it in Russian. None of us knew that Wilson could speak Russian, but under Moscow's heady influence he had been convinced that he could, or at least read it from a phonetic script. So these two senior diplomats had spent the night translating the speech into Russian. In itself, this was not too difficult, but they knew that Wilson couldn't actually read the Russian alphabet, nor indeed could Mr Garrett's machine cope with it. So Brimelow and Morgan then had to transliterate their text back into Latin characters. Even that wasn't the end of the process. A standard letter-for-letter transliteration would give the PM little idea of how to pronounce the words or where to place the all-important stress. A phonetic version had to be devised and written down. These were the stages that Brimelow and Morgan had to go through just for the first few words:

Original

Dear Russian friends! I have come to the Soviet Union …

Russian translation

Дорогие русские друзья! Я приехал в Советский Союз …

Standard transliteration

Dorogie russkie druzya! Ya priekhal v Sovetskiy Soyuz …

Brimelow/Morgan phonetic version

Daragíyeh róoskiyeh droozyáh! Yah preeyékhal ver Savyétskee Sayóoz …

The new text was handed to Mr Garrett, who had the day to transfer it on to his tapes. In the evening the whole party sped off to the Ostankino television studio, where the machine was waiting, eagerly photographed from all angles by the Russians. It was a conical shape and looked to me like one of the Daleks from the new Dr Who series: I kept expecting it to wander off the set. Wilson sat down confidently in front of it for a rehearsal and … disaster! He couldn't read the unfamiliar text without his glasses. He never wore glasses in public and he wouldn't do so now, he asserted. There followed a long negotiation, which was largely between Wilson and himself, since only he could decide whether his priority was to 'get himself across' or preserve his public image. But the Russian speakers around him tactfully nudged him towards abandoning the attempt – even with his glasses on his Russian could barely be understood. It wasn't entirely his fault. The teleprompter's small screen couldn't accommodate many of the long words in the phonetic transliteration. Mr Garrett had had to wrap them round and, having no Russian, had had to guess where to break the longer words. So what Wilson was trying to read looked something like this:

DARAGÍYEH RÓOSKIYEH
DROOZYÁH! YAH PREE-
YÉKHAL VER SAVYÉT-
SKEE SAYÓOZ ...

Eventually a compromise was reached: he would read the first and last few sentences, glasses on, in Russian, and the rest in English, where his familiarity with the text meant that he didn't need to see it all that clearly. So 90 per cent of Brimelow's and Morgan's overnight work was binned, and Mr Garrett was set to pasting back most of the old text on the tape.

Meanwhile another publicity exercise, this time for the British viewer, was getting under way. Wilson had arranged for Panorama, at that time the BBC's flagship current affairs programme, to be transmitted that evening live from Moscow. The entire Panorama team was in the studio, where the presenter dramatically announced: *This is Panorama, broadcasting live from Moscow!* The content was less dramatic: a series of interviews with Wilson and his ministers against a background picture of the Kremlin. It must have been around midnight when it was over, Moscow being three hours ahead of London, but poor Mr Garrett still hadn't finished his task. Searching around for something to do, Wilson roused Robert Carvel, political editor of *The Evening Standard*, from his hotel bed, and I was despatched to fetch him in my little red *Moskvich*. Striding up and down the studio with Carvel, Wilson talked incessantly until it was time for him to disappear into the sound-proof recording studio, his speech finally being ready.

By the time it was broadcast, the whole circus was back in London. Raili and I settled down a little apprehensively to watch it on our new television. Against the backdrop of a large Union Jack, an owlish figure in glasses appeared, speaking in a language that had never been heard before, while the voice-over interpreter remained tactfully silent. Despite having rehearsed his few Russian sentences repeatedly, once Wilson was in the studio alone with his teleprompter he muffed them. It was a relief when the glasses came off and he settled into a homely fireside chat that probably had the intended effect on anyone still watching, since he was looking straight at us, thanks to the teleprompter. After a while, though, he screwed up his eyes, stumbled over his words, fumbled for his glasses and finally unburdened himself of the tattered remains of his original attempt to get himself across to the Russian people in their own language.

I was appalled at the waste of time, energy and money that had gone into this exhibition of political hubris. I also felt vaguely let down when I saw Wilson's late night briefing appear under Carvel's byline as an independent think-piece with occasional references to 'sources close to the prime minister'. I was new and had a lot to learn. But I was mollified by a nice thank-you letter from Mary Wilson, accompanied by a signed photograph. She must have written hundreds of them during her time as prime minister's wife. But I couldn't imagine her as less than sincere, and I treasured them.

That was the only occasion when Mary Wilson accompanied her husband to Moscow, and it meant that my involvement in his next two visits was minimal. Wilson was back in July 1966, ostensibly for the British Industrial Exhibition, but in fact to pursue his dream of ending the Vietnam War by linking the Americans and the North Vietnamese via himself and the Russians. He told Kosygin that there could be occasions when the Americans might find it preferable to make urgent points to the Russians through a third party such as the United Kingdom rather than directly, and vice versa. Wilson had in mind a permanently manned telephone link, which would have required massive funds and an inexhaustible supply of competent Russian speakers, but the idea never died. It ended up as a teleprinter 'hot line' between London and Moscow that was indeed permanently manned by GCHQ linguists. It must have got under way fairly quickly, as before the end of my tour I was despatched to one of Moscow's main railway stations to take delivery of the kit that would be installed at the Moscow end of the line.

When Wilson came for the third time, towards the end of January 1968, we were within weeks of saying good-bye to Moscow. Although I was standing by to interpret, the main outcome of the visit for me was domestic. 'You will have gathered that Mr Wilson didn't bring much back from Moscow,' I wrote to my parents, 'but he did bring two suitcases of mine, which I think made his visit worth the while.'

In the interval, we had had two visits from Wilson's pugnacious new foreign secretary, George Brown, the man for whom the phrase 'tired and emotional', meaning 'drunk and abusive' was coined. His appointment in August 1966 had sent shivers down British and Russian diplomatic spines alike. For the British it was the enormous chip on his shoulder, which got in the way whenever he felt he was being talked down to by an old school Foreign Office type. Our ambassador, Sir Geoffrey Harrison, was an obvious target, and he soon felt the lash of Brown's tongue on the latter's first visit in October 1966. No doubt in response to some measured advice, which it was Sir Geoffrey's job to give, Brown turned on him and shouted: 'You shut up, or I'll post you to the Yemen!' Although this was said in a small gathering, Brown's words reverberated round the embassy and found their way into our Christmas entertainment, expertly woven into a song by Brian Fall's wife Delmar, with the refrain:

It's off to the Yemen you'll go, my boy,
It's off to the Yemen you'll go!

For their part, the Russians had been wary of Brown ever since he had had a stormy exchange of insults in April 1956 with the equally touchy and hot-tempered Khrushchev over the fate of social democrats in Eastern Europe under Communist rule. But all went smoothly during his visits to Moscow, and on the second one, in May 1967, he may have 'got across' to the Russian people rather better than Harold Wilson, since he was allowed a press conference with Soviet journalists and a speech to an invited audience at the House of Friendship, a first for a Western dignitary, as far as could be ascertained. I was called on to interpret for Brown as he read his speech. Or rather, to read it out paragraph by paragraph in Russian, since the speech had already been translated in London and, apart from a few phrases at the start, Brown stuck to his text. He did have an official interpreter, a Miss E Shapiro, British-born, but with native Russian. She was a professional freelance interpreter, whom the FCO had hired for the occasion. She was being given a rest while Brown made his speech, it was said, but I had been told that Brown didn't want a woman reading out his speech. He wanted a man and a recognisably British man at that (i.e. not a Soviet interpreter). I suppose he wanted the words that came out of my mouth to sound as if they were coming out of his, but he didn't make Wilson's mistake of thinking he could enunciate them himself. When it came to

His master's voice: the author reading out George Brown's speech while his official interpreter, Miss E Shapiro, awaits her turn.

Below: the audience. Front row from the left: Joe Dobbs, Head of the Russian Secretariat, British Embassy, Moscow; Keith Matthews, Minister, British Embassy, Moscow; Peter Hayman, Assistant Under Secretary of State, Foreign Office; Mikhail Smirnovsky, Soviet Ambassador, London; Sir Geoffrey Harrison, British Ambassador, Moscow

questions, real interpreting skills were required; Miss Shapiro jumped to her feet and I discreetly retired.

The British had not previously felt the need for professional interpreters in Anglo-Soviet diplomatic exchanges, choosing competent linguists from available staff, as did the Russians. The model for all later interpreters was A H Birse (1889-1967). He was impeccably British, but spoke better Russian that many native speakers, having been educated in pre-revolutionary Russia, where his family had run a business, as he himself did until driven out by the revolution. Birse was back in Moscow during the war, as a member of the British Military Mission, when Winston Churchill paid his first visit to Stalin in the summer of 1942. Churchill had been dispirited by Stalin's nagging him to open a 'second front', i.e. invade German-occupied France to relieve the pressure on the Soviet Union, and was inclined to cut short his visit. But he was persuaded to have one more go at Stalin and secured a late night meeting. Birse was called in at short notice to interpret, as the Embassy's interpreter was unwell. Birse had never met Churchill, or indeed done any interpreting other than on military subjects, but he played a crucial role in helping Churchill find a rapport with Stalin at the meeting, which turned into a late night, alcohol-fuelled banquet of the sort Stalin loved. 'Are you getting me across all right? ... I think you are doing very well,' Churchill scribbled on a piece of paper that he passed across to Birse, and the next day the ambassador noted that Churchill was confident that Birse had 'got him across.' Birse had won Churchill's confidence and was called upon for all the wartime high-level meetings after that. He was followed by Hugh Lunghi, the son of a British consul, who had learnt Russian at his Anglo-Russian mother's knee. Lunghi was also a member of the British Military Mission and after the war one of the first members of the Russian Secretariat. Birse, Lunghi and their successors did far more than the basic job of turning their principal's English into Russian. They assessed nuances in the speeches of the Russians that might have been lost in translation; caught exchanges within the Soviet delegation that were not meant for our ears; commented from knowledge and experience on atmosphere and body language; and made a record of those sometimes crucial exchanges which only the interpreters had witnessed.

The practice of using gifted amateurs from the Foreign Service's own resources continued. In my time they included Marcus Wheeler, Geoff Murrell, John Morgan and, above all, Ted Orchard. He came out with Michael Stewart in 1965 and with Wilson on his third visit in 1968. Rodric Braithwaite, First Secretary Commercial, was a natural choice to interpret for Wilson on what was ostensibly a commercial visit in July 1966. This ad hoc system may have been put under strain by the sudden rush of high-level exchanges, for when Wilson arrived in Moscow for his first major visit in February 1966 his interpreter was Miss Shapiro, as she was for George Brown for his two visits.

It was around this time that I was asked by Anthony Williams, my Head of Chancery, if I would be interested in a job that was to be created in the Foreign Office: conference interpreter in Russian. He gave me to understand that the initiative came from the prime minister himself. Anticipating ever closer and more frequent contacts with the Soviet leadership, Wilson felt he needed a regular interpreter who was both up to the highest professional standards, but also part of his team. As a freelance interpreter, Miss Shapiro clearly couldn't meet the second requirement. Informally, and a little mischievously, it was being said that the prime minister was uncomfortable with a woman interpreter. He felt he could only achieve his goal of contributing to peace in Vietnam if he could take Kosygin aside for a 'man-to-man' talk, which could just as well happen in the gents' toilet as anywhere else. What if he was deprived of his interpreter at this critical moment?

I was enthusiastic, despite warnings from Anthony Williams and from the Head of Personnel Department when on a visit to Moscow. The job, they said, would be demanding and draining. It would require a high level of concentration over long periods of time, as well as travel at short notice and unsocial hours. But it played to my strengths as a linguist and, yes, for all my scorn at the hubris of Wilson and Brown, I was attracted by the thought of being at their side in those vital talks they envisaged. The Russians had their star interpreter in the person of Viktor Sukhodrev, who had learnt his flawless English in London in the 1940s as the son of an official at the Soviet Trade Delegation and who was always seen at the shoulder of Khrushchev and later Brezhnev and Kosygin. Why shouldn't we have such a person?

I was given the impression that the job was mine for the asking, and once I had put in my application in May 1967 there was talk of ending my tour early to start training. But it turned out that the FCO was in parallel advertising for a fully-fledged conference interpreter from outside, who would then be taken on as a permanent member of staff without the delay involved in training. So my application was filed away.

Meanwhile, the revolving door between Research Department in London and the Russian Secretariat in Moscow began to turn again at the end of 1967 and beginning of 1968. David Miller, who had filled the gap between Tony Bishop and me in 1965, was back for his first substantive posting; and Geoff Murrell, whom I had got to know while he was on his first Moscow tour and I was a student there, was coming out to replace me. Strictly speaking, my tour should have ended in December 1967 – two one-year tours plus six weeks for home leave – but I had negotiated an extension to take us over most of the winter. Difficult though Moscow winters were, we were well settled and felt better off there than house-hunting in England just before Christmas.

We left Moscow on 9th February 1968 by our favourite route on the overnight train to Finland, with a good embassy crowd and my personal KGB 'tail' on the platform to see us off, but without any deep emotions. I was anxious to get back home. Raili was pregnant, and finding somewhere to live on our return had become an urgent task. I left Raili and Karin in Artjärvi for a couple of weeks and hurried back to England. Marjatta remained in Moscow with another embassy family.

Knowing that we wanted to continue living in Twickenham and what price bracket we had in mind, my parents had already done the groundwork and narrowed the choice to two: a neat, modern terraced house tucked away by the River Crane in Campbell Close, with Whitton the nearest station, and a similar-sized 1930s terraced house in Marble Hill Close, opposite beautiful Marble Hill Park. Both were good for a young family, well away from the danger of fast-moving traffic, but No. 49 Marble Hill Close easily won out. It had a large hall, with room to store a pram, and it was in a prime location. It had been advertised as close to shops, buses and station (St Margaret's), but a further advantage was that it was much nearer than Campbell Close to my parents, on whom we leant heavily for advice, physical assistance (I remember us all carrying the turf for our small lawn roll by roll through the house on a soaking wet day) and the use of their car. We bought it, this time with a proper mortgage, for around £6,000.

I worried of course that I couldn't afford it, although I had just been promoted to Research Assistant Grade II with a salary increase from £1,100 to £1,700 per annum. I also had the prospect of a princely £2,500 ahead of me if I got the interpreter job, but the whole affair was moving so slowly that I wisely ignored that carrot. Even when translated roughly into the values of some 50 years later, the figures (£86,000 for the house and £24,000 for my salary) seem modest. And so they were. The houses in this now prized area of Twickenham could still be bought by middle-ranking civil servants. We had got our foot on the housing ladder fairly easily, to find ourselves propelled upwards by inflation in house prices to the point where we couldn't now contemplate buying the place we live in.

After a frustrating wait, as the previous owner prevaricated about completing the deal, we finally, took possession in May. A flurry of work ensued. We had the wall dividing front and back rooms taken down to make a big living area, and I laid an oak parquet floor – a good tongue and groove design that didn't have to be laid on an absolutely even base. We carpeted the upstairs with an incredibly rough sisal carpet from John Lewis – my first venture into hire purchase. Outside I made an impressive garden hut out of our Moscow packing cases. They had been recycled from wooden boxes containing equipment sent out to the embassy addressed to Her Britannic Majesty's Ambassador, so the side of my garden hut was emblazoned with the words 'HBM AMBASSADOR MOSCOW'.

Other endeavours were less successful. I was always looking to save money and tended to undertake tasks that were beyond me. Having decided to decorate the exterior of the house myself, I stabbed a coat of white emulsion on the difficult pebble dash walls, but baulked at the prospect of doing all the window frames, so got in our local painter to give an estimate. 'And the pebble dash looks as if it needs a couple of coats,' he commented innocently, looking at my recent handiwork. 'Would you like me to do that too?' Dejected, I had to accept.

Marjatta joined us from Moscow to help smooth our transition from a one- to two-child family. In Moscow, we had been NHS patients, but privileged ones as we couldn't in practice go out and fend for ourselves. So using the 'pull' that the situation gave him, our embassy doctor was able to book Raili into the most prestigious maternity hospital in London, Queen Charlotte's, close by in Ravenscourt Park, Hammersmith. With the baby apparently a week or so overdue Raili took herself there on the District Line, small suitcase in hand, to have it induced. She met a friend on the way who asked her where she was going. 'I'm going to have a baby,' she replied, brightly, and was a little dismayed at her friend apparently regarding this as a commonplace activity.

Queen Charlotte's was ahead of its time in allowing fathers to attend the birth, and I was soon contentedly sitting by Raili's bed in her single room, entrusted by the duty nurse to regulate the drip that would stimulate contractions. Unfortunately the nurse on the next shift hadn't caught the spirit of the times and hustled me out. It was quite out of order for me to be regulating the drip, or to be in the room at all, she muttered. In an instant I was reduced from competent, caring helper to anxious father-to-be, nervously pacing up and down the corridor. So I took the sensible option of driving home for Marjatta's spaghetti Bolognese before going back to the hospital towards evening to resume my vigil. I found Raili's room empty: she was in the delivery ward, but I was advised not to go there as she was in distress. 'All the more reason for me to be with her,' I argued, adding that I was not new to childbirth, and from a pretty close angle at that. 'Ah,' said the nurse, visibly relaxing, 'then she's acting normal.' I was equipped with white coat, face mask and cap before being escorted into the ward, where I found Raili, as the expressive phrase has it, 'in labour'. They wanted to put a gas mask of some sort on her when the time came to push, as she was not performing very well, but Raili had a horror of things on her face, and I persuaded them to let me issue the 'pant' and 'push' orders directly into her ear, which she executed so effectively that the baby popped out quite quickly. All this in front of a semi-circle of a dozen trainee midwives. They had been summoned to witness a baby making a slightly unusual, nose first, entry into the world. Masks off, the duty doctor asked me who I was; he was puzzled by the unfamiliar face. 'You seemed to know what you were doing, so I assumed you were on the staff,' he said shaking my hand after I had told him I was the proud father, and my already flushed face glowed even more brightly. I was restored to my position of competent helper and left alone to look after Raili once the staff had whipped the new baby away. My job was to stop the comatose Raili falling off the narrow delivery bed; it seemed a long time before someone came to relieve me and I was able to dash to the phone to announce: 'It's a boy!'

It had been a miserable, cold summer, dry but with a persistent east wind driving grey clouds across the sky. Every morning when I woke up to see the ugly willow in our back garden bending in the same direction I knew that there would be no change. But on that night towards ten o'clock, as I drove home, I saw a break in the clouds and the moon shining through, a magical conclusion to the day. It was 8th August 1968 ('eight-eight-sixty-eight, who-do-we-appreci-ate,' as we used to chant many a time in later years). A long but happy day, like Karin's birth three years earlier.

We had names up our sleeves: Ruth for a girl and Colin for a boy, so Colin it was. The name was in the family – it had belonged to my seafaring paternal grandfather Captain Colin Nicholson – and it would be easy for Finns. We hadn't been able to think of a second name for Karin, so Colin didn't get one either. Of course Karin was jealous, despite our elaborate preparations on Raili's return from hospital to reassure her that she was still number one. But she relented once Colin was old enough to be propped up in her play house and become a guest at her tea parties.

On 21st August I realised I had completely forgotten to register Colin's birth and was now worrying that I had missed the boat and somehow he would never become a properly documented person. Years behind the iron curtain had engendered in me a rather craven attitude towards bureaucratic procedures – I always expected to be caught out. As I drove urgently to Queen Charlotte's in my parents' car I ignored the billboards outside my local station announcing: SOVIET TROOPS INVADE CZECHOSLOVAKIA. 'They wouldn't be so silly,' I muttered to myself, not the only time I attributed to the Soviet leadership a dose of common sense that events were to show they totally lacked. Or maybe the wish was father to the thought, as I was in domestic mode at that time and really didn't want to be bothered with international crises. It would be years before I caught up with what had really happened in Czechoslovakia.

With Marjatta around as well as my parents, Raili wasn't too stretched, and for post-natal therapy took up serious study of Russian. She had returned from Moscow fired with an enthusiasm to master the language and to this day has never lost it. She had even carried Nina Potapova's turgid textbook to Queen Charlotte's in her little suitcase. But once the 1968 autumn term started she enrolled at an evening class in Kingston that was teaching the BBC's excellent Second Year Russian course, devised by Paddy O'Toole of Essex University, whom we'd got to know while he was on a visit to Moscow. In Kingston she used the language laboratory to do the drills, while at home she listened to the lessons themselves on Radio 3 and 4. Despite all the difficulties of travel to the USSR at that time, there was still a residue of enthusiasm for the country and its culture that had flourished in the years of the 'thaw' in the early 1960s.

All the while the office was continuing at snail's pace to pursue its fallback plan to appoint a trainee interpreter in Russian. It was only that same 21st August 1968 that Personnel Department formally responded to my application of more than a year previously, acknowledging that they had failed to find a top level Russian interpreter and asking if I was still interested in the junior post. Tony Bishop had also been approached, and he and I sat language tests in November 1968. It took the office a further three months to decide that they couldn't choose between us and to offer the job to us jointly. There was an air of unreality to all this. In the three years that had passed since the idea had first taken shape the élan that had marked Wilson's and Brown's visits to Moscow had faded, as had the so-called 'Kosygin spirit' that had lingered after the Soviet prime minister's successful visit to London in February 1967. Early in 1968 George Brown had told his officials that there were too many ministerial visits to Moscow with too little purpose, and now Czechoslovakia had stopped the traffic entirely for the foreseeable future. It didn't look as though there would be much work for one Russian interpreter, let alone two. That, however, was not our concern. Apart from the intrinsic appeal of the job, with our young families to support we could hardly turn up our noses at the excellent terms: promotion to the equivalent of Grade 5A, that is, first secretary in the A Branch, and a salary increase of about a third, from our current £1,700 to £2,600.

I had naively assumed that we would do our training as full time students in some proper academic setting, such as the Central London Polytechnic (Westminster University from 1992), which ran a well regarded Russian interpreting course. The original job description had said enticingly, but vaguely, that training might take place 'abroad'. In the event we were offered just a short evening course at the Linguists' Club in Niddry Lodge, off Kensington High Street. It seemed a bit of a come-down, since the course was designed to teach interpreting techniques as such, without regard to the languages involved. It was also onerous for Tony, living in Kent. Once a week he would come home from work with me for supper, after which I'd drive him to Kensington and he would take a late train home after the class.

It turned out to be a worthwhile course. The Linguists' Club had been founded by Teddy Pilley, born Ary Thadee Pilichowski, the son of prominent Polish Jewish immigrants. He himself ran our course, which he preferred to call a working group: we were, after all, in a club. Pilley was dedicated to improving the status of interpreters and to this end had helped to found the Association of International Conference Interpreters. He accepted the need for the modern variant of simultaneous interpreting at large conferences, when the interpreters sat in sound-proof booths listening through earphones to speech in one language and reproducing it simultaneously in another. But he maintained that this method limited the interpreter's role; if the speaker rambled, the interpreter had to ramble with him. Pilley's interest was in consecutive interpreting, which was what we would be doing. Here, he would claim, if the speaker rambled or was in some other way unclear or illogical, the interpreter could actually improve on his principal by repackaging the sometimes large chunks of speech that he was putting into the other language.

With this lofty goal to aim at, learning to interpret from English to English was itself a challenge. We had to make sense of what was being said, making just the briefest of notes to use as prompts, and to know where and how to break into the speaker's flow to get our interpretation in, sometimes to the speaker's irritation. One of the ambassadors for whom Tony later worked on arms control talks admitted that he could never reconcile himself to stopping for interpretation, even though he knew that without it his words were wasted. He would introduce Tony to the other side as 'my interrupter'. Former Soviet president Mikhail Gorbachev was incorrigible in this respect. In a speech he gave in London in 2004 he just would not stop the flow, so his interpreter had to resort to simultaneous interpreting. The audience, lacking the earphones that would allow them to concentrate on one or other of the two languages, had to put up with both at the same time as Gorbachev and his interpreter competed ever more loudly, each trying to be heard over the other.

For all the value of Pilley's working group, Tony and I felt the need for more tuition in contemporary Russian, especially the current affairs vocabulary. Of course, we had our daily diet of *Pravda* and *Izvestiya*, but they spoke 'Sovietese', blocks of standard formulations weighted towards Soviet ideology. We wanted to be able to reflect Western speech and ways of thinking, but in a language that would come across to Russians as their own. The office met our request for some private tuition handsomely in the person of Aziz Ulug-Zade. Ethnically Uzbek but Moscow educated, he was entirely Russian in outlook and later russified his surname to Ulugov. He was about our age and had defected as recently as 1967 while interpreting for a Soviet delegation in India. It surprised me that the security-conscious British authorities were willing to entrust two of their officials to the care of such a recent defector, especially as Moscow University's prestigious Institute of Asian and African

Studies, where Aziz took his degree, was well known for its output of intelligence officers as well as scholars and diplomats. But one didn't ask questions, and although we lost touch with him, I was glad to see that the 1993 edition of the Oxford Russian Dictionary acknowledged him as a valuable adviser. We would visit Aziz in his Earl's Court flat once a week, in office hours this time, where together we would work out the best ways of putting into Russian articles in *The Economist* and any awkward English phrases that we had come across during the week.

Thus our training, though modest, was fruitful, the more so as we were able to put it into instant practice with interpreting assignments. The era of high-level visits was over. But despite the general freeze in Anglo-Soviet relations after Czechoslovakia, some of the initiatives of sunnier times survived. One of them was the inaugural, and in the event only, meeting of the Anglo-Soviet Consultative Committee. It was in essence a talking shop between policy-makers on both sides in the arts, sciences and commerce, looking for areas where despite our differing political systems we and the Russians could co-operate. Our side had cancelled two meetings, planned for 1968, but was now ready to revive the idea. From Tony's and my narrow perspective that was a good thing, as when the Committee finally met in April 1970 we were more or less fully trained and eager to put our skills to the test.

The weekend meeting started inauspiciously. On Friday 3rd April a coach deposited the two delegations at the British Transport Staff

College on the outskirts of Woking. Here they were suitably wined and dined and settled into comfortable chairs to enjoy a talk and slide show from Sir John Hunt, who had led the expedition that put Hillary and Tensing on top of Mount Everest in 1953. It was an embarrassing occasion, as in the darkened room his even tones – he must have given the lecture hundreds of times before – had a soporific effect, and he was soon finding it hard to make himself heard over the loud snoring of the assembled well fed and watered grandees. The next two days were all committees and subcommittees, with Tony and me interpreting as necessary and amusing ourselves by cocking an ear to the informal talk of the Russians among themselves. British newspapers were reporting an air crash in the Soviet Union, and I overheard the leader of the Soviet delegation, Deputy Foreign Minister Kozyrev, checking with his colleagues whether it had yet been reported in the Soviet press. He didn't want to reveal knowledge of something he wasn't supposed to know.

Tony and I had divided the interpreting 'plums' meticulously between us, and it had fallen to me to interpret for the leader of the UK delegation, Sir Humphrey Trevelyan, in the final plenary session. The delegates were noisily chatting among themselves and not responding to Sir Humphrey's calls to order, so to make sure they took notice I raised my voice. I was following one of Pilley's rather self-aggrandising maxims that sometimes the interpreter had to assert his principal's authority if the latter was too self-effacing to do so. I don't remember whether my peremptory tone had any effect on the company in general, but it certainly startled Sir Humphrey, who took an early opportunity discreetly to replace me with Tony, whom he knew well, having been his ambassador in Moscow. I was put out, of course, but not for long. In the first place Tony was not one to take undue advantage of this unexpected plum falling in his lap, and in the second place I learnt a salutary lesson: if the principal loses confidence in his interpreter, it is just too bad and not worth dwelling on. Miss Shapiro must have understood that when she was stood down in Moscow. I was anyway back in the saddle early the following week, interpreting for the most senior FCO civil servant, the Permanent Under-Secretary Sir Denis Greenhill, in his official talks with Kozyrev.

The Consultative Committee died a natural death, but before doing so it spawned a number of specialised Working Groups that provided us with more interpreting opportunities. I worked with a delegation from the Soviet planning committee *Gosplan* in London, and early in the summer of 1970 went to Moscow with the British delegation to the cumbersomely named Anglo-Soviet Medical Equipment and Instrumentation Working Group. It was a relaxed visit – I recall a long lunch in the sun under the awnings of a restaurant on the outskirts of Moscow. The British team were representatives of small businesses who had been cajoled into the trip by an energetic man from the Ministry of Health. He had assured them the trip would open up business opportunities. In the event the Russians were interested only in the man who brought a collection of ceramic dentures with him – the era when the flash of gold characterised every Russian smile was passing. For our part, we were interested in the Russians' display of their latest achievements, which were frighteningly powerful, like the ultrasound machine that shattered kidney stones. Just as we were proud of the 'Made in Britain' label, so they were of their own products. They had an even more patriotic term for them in Russian: *otechestvenny*, meaning produce of the fatherland. Unfortunately their otherwise impeccable interpreter rendered it as 'home made'. Some of the products certainly looked that way – we found ourselves in a ward of latter day Frankenstein's monsters, the steel pinnings for their bone replacements protruding out of their skin in such a way that I half expected the duty surgeon to be doing his rounds with spanner in hand. 'Our designers are first and foremost engineers,' said our guide, somewhat apologetically.

Air services, the subject of a ten-day trip to Moscow in December 1969, provided a drier subject and a tougher interpreting assignment. Earlier in the year the Russians had relaxed their long-standing ban on foreign aircraft flying over Siberia. Our long-haul operator BOAC, the British Overseas Airways Corporation, was anxious to secure a direct route to Tokyo, which would shorten by several hours its existing route going the other way round the world via Alaska. I spent many hours before the trip mugging up on the terminology and the political background.

I didn't need to understand the issues in depth so long as I understood the unfamiliar terminology. I had to concentrate on keeping on the same wavelength as Ray Le Goy, a senior official from the Board of Trade, who led the delegation and with whom I worked intensively for ten days. Small, mercurial, camp, with a goatee beard and a wispy lock of hair covering, or more often failing to cover his balding head, Ray looked out of place among the macho ex-pilots that made up the large delegations on both sides. But his own supreme self-assurance had the effect of making the rest of us self-conscious. My embarrassing moment came after a reception at the British Embassy when Ray decided to walk back with me to our hotel, the recently built *Rossiya*, facing the Kremlin. As the icy blast from the Moscow river hit us Ray realised that, hatless and in town shoes, he was woefully underdressed, so he drew his scarf over his head and put his arm firmly through mine so as not to slip on the icy pavement. From behind it must have looked as if a young man was supporting his elderly grandmother, but there was clearly something odd about us, since every Russian who walked past turned to look back and was surprised to see that this *babushka* had a prominent beard. I did my best to look as if this was the natural order of things as Ray, unconcerned, minced along at my side, bearded chin wagging animatedly. Sartorially, a few days later the laugh was on me. As the negotiations spanned a weekend our hosts flew the entire delegation on a recreational visit to Tashkent, capital of Uzbekistan, in a massive *Ilyushin* with four twin propellers and individual cabins furnished with beds. When we staggered back to the plane after an indulgent farewell dinner I was wearing the Uzbek national headdress that had been presented to me and which seemed entirely appropriate to the venue. My *tubeteika* felt distinctly less appropriate when, still wearing it, I stepped out of the plane into the freezing Moscow air, with no idea where my Russian fur hat had got to. Thankfully our kind Uzbek hosts had found it and rushed it to the plane.

Ray Le Goy had a quicksilver mind and enjoyed the intellectual challenge of negotiations, firing out one idea after another. That, he explained, was how he negotiated with the Americans, who would return his fire in like manner until agreement was reached. He had never negotiated with Russians, who couldn't understand what he was up to. After several fruitless days the Deputy Minister of Aviation leading the Soviet delegation, a stolid former air force pilot, summoned Le Goy (with me at his side) for a private dressing-down, threatening to call off the negotiations unless the British side acted more responsibly. From then on things moved towards the end game, and our delegation began to melt away once each member was satisfied that his own interests had been met. In the end only Ray and I were left to agree the final wording; we arrived back late on 18th December, far too close to Christmas for my comfort. I never got the measure of Ray Le Goy, nor, I think, did the rest of our delegation. We had assumed he was gay, but he surprised us at a reunion some months later by turning up with a stunning Jamaican wife at his side.

I had returned to find both children poorly, as well as my mother, whom Raili had nonetheless had to call upon to drive them to the doctor. It was at that point that Raili realised she would have to abandon her disdain for the actual business of driving. She passed her test first time. We had bought our car, a blue Morris Minor called Winnie, from my brother Robin, but as long as I was the only driver it sat most of the week idle in front of our house. In order to give it some exercise I took to starting my daily commute by driving to Kew Gardens, but soon gave up the idea when I realised that driving slowly back in the rush hour rather than striding purposefully home was the reason for my increasing tiredness and bad temper in the evenings.

For despite the novelty of interpreting Tony and I still spent most of our time on the Kremlinological treadmill. Tony was building up expertise on Soviet defence and disarmament policy while interpreting in Geneva at the negotiations for a treaty on the non-proliferation of nuclear weapons, while I was studying the 'Brezhnev doctrine', the ideology under which the Russians justified their invasion of Czechoslovakia.

It was at this point that I first got wind of a posting back to Moscow. I didn't welcome the idea. We were enjoying bringing up our young family in familiar surroundings. Karin was assimilating well at Orleans Infants School, which we could reach without crossing a road. So well in fact that she had just decided to give up speaking Finnish. Twickenham was not the cosmopolitan place it would later become, and heads would turn when Karin spoke to Raili in Finnish, especially if their conversation appeared to refer to someone else in the company. But the tipping point seems to have been some incident at school, when Karin may have found her words coming out in Finnish and everyone laughed. At all events, that was it; she didn't speak Finnish again. I took it as the natural course of events, not fully understanding what a wrench it was for Raili to have to abandon the language in which she had spoken to her daughter from birth. But Raili wisely accepted the situation, not taking the advice of well-meaning friends who advocated speaking Finnish at breakfast, English at lunch and so on. It would never have worked with us. So Colin, unlike Karin, began as an English speaker.

The post I was being offered was Head of the Russian Secretariat. This was an unexpected advance. But in my working life expulsions and visa refusals played as much of a role as any career plans, and this seems to have been one of those occasions. My boss as Head of the Secretariat, Joe Dobbs, had left Moscow in mid-1968 to become Consul General in Zagreb, but his intended replacement, Michael Duncan, whom I had known in my student year while he was on an earlier Moscow tour, had been refused a visa. A man with a profound knowledge of Russian culture and well-known as a translator, his extra-curricular social activities among the intelligentsia may have got under the Soviet authorities' skin. Michael would have provided excellent support to the new ambassador, Sir Duncan Wilson, a scholar diplomat who had earlier been Director of Research and who had crowned his last posting as ambassador to Yugoslavia with a book on one of the founding fathers of that country, Vuk Karadžić. I met Sir Duncan in 1970 when he was in London for a meeting. His posting was nearing its end, but he still wanted to convince the sceptics in Whitehall that there were more signs of change for the better in the Soviet Union than they would acknowledge. He wanted to put lines out to the younger generation of intellectuals and technocrats, but implied that Bob Longmire, who had been posted instead of Michael, hadn't quite met his expectations. Bob was an old Soviet hand from Research Department, but he had switched his focus to the Asian subcontinent and had little recent experience of the Soviet Union. Sitting on a table and swinging his legs – such a different man from my previous ambassador – Sir Duncan suggested that being younger and more familiar with the Soviet Union today I could do something along the lines he envisaged. Reluctant as I was to move away from my cosy domesticity, this was an offer I could hardly refuse, particularly as Ted Orchard, to whom the post had seemed to belong as of right, had been promoted to Director of Research, so was no longer in the running.

What about interpreting, my main focus over the last year or so? I could pursue such opportunities as they arose equally well from Moscow as from London, I was told. Indeed, I was already in Moscow when on 24th February 1971 my appointment as interpreter along with Tony Bishop was finally confirmed. Ironically, my interpreting days were by then effectively over, as I was to find out. For Tony, however, the appointment marked the start of a distinguished career that would take him to a position corresponding perfectly to the original plan – a skilled, experienced and valued consort of prime ministers and other British dignitaries in their dealings with a succession of Soviet and Russian leaders.

So on 4th January 1971 we were in the air again on our way to Moscow. We had let our house to the son of a vicar who lived opposite my parents. He wasn't very keen, as he felt the house was too big for him and his young wife, but we dropped the rent to a derisory amount in order to secure a tenant whom we knew and could check up on. So under considerable pressure from his family and us he reluctantly signed up. He was never at ease with the deal, and six months later he would exercise his right to end the contract. As events transpired, that was a boon.

Five

Moscow 1971: 'Activities Incompatible'

R aili and I remember Christmas 1970 as a time when we looked wistfully through the windows of the houses in our tranquil close and saw people just like us living their ordinary family lives, snug among their modest Christmas decorations. We should have been doing the same, but we were long since packed up and prepared for a posting that we hadn't particularly sought. And winter in Moscow was at its most uncompromising when we arrived in a blizzard.

The travails of the move were forgotten, however, as soon as we found ourselves in the familiar surroundings of the *Sadovo-Samotechnaya* block, where we had started in 1965. We were pampered. For a start, we had a larger flat overlooking the courtyard as well as the ring road. It wasn't officially reserved for the Head of the Russian Secretariat, but some flats tended to go with the job. During our first tour it had housed my boss Joe Dobbs and his family, and it housed his successor, my predecessor Bob Longmire. Together with the flat came the Dobbs' former maid Nina, 'comfortable and round', as I described her in a letter home. She was an eager and talented cook; despite having no English she quickly absorbed the Cordon Bleu course that my mother was sending out to Raili in instalments. The embassy still enjoyed a long lunch hour, so Nina regularly provided a full scale family lunch that quickly made us comfortable and round as well.

We were soon into our new life. By the end of our first week Karin was being ferried in an embassy car to mornings at the Anglo-American school. A week or so later we were out skiing on the Lenin Hills, our blue Ford Cortina having been delivered from England and four sets of cross-country skis and boots from Finland. With Marjatta again joining us from Finland our family set-up was complete. Raili was freed from everyday chores and resumed her ballet classes and Russian studies. For still more intellectual stimulus she embarked on a rather self-serving piece of academic research designed to show that all the rivers in the north of Russia had Finnish roots to their names, so the Finns must have got there first.

While Raili was pursuing her project I would drop her off at the Lenin Library on my way to the embassy. One of the two cars following us would stop and disgorge as many as three or four sleuths to track her into the building and, presumably, find out from the staff exactly what this diplomatic wife was up to in the professors' reading room – the same room where I had spent many academically unfocused hours as a postgraduate student.

The embassy looked much the same as when we had left it three years previously; I had also been back a couple of times on interpreting trips, and the 'militiaman' on the gate greeted me with a shy smile of recognition when I first reappeared. The embassy's internal geography had changed, though. The Russian Secretariat was no longer housed in the wing to my left as I came out of the entrance of the main embassy building. In that wing the doctor was still on the first floor, but under him now was what we called the Russian Admin – locally employed Russians who looked after our requirements for tickets, passes and so on. They had moved across the front courtyard from the wing on the right of the entrance to make way for the Army, Navy and Air Attachés.

I found it odd that the highly secure operation of these attachés should be housed in a wing whose outer wall was on the boundary of the embassy's territory. The Russians could easily drill into it in order to plant their listening devices. But I figured out what must have happened (one didn't ask). In October 1964, before our first tour, a posse of surprisingly prompt Soviet 'firemen' had battled with embassy staff to get to the scene of a fire that had mysteriously broken out in the upper storey of that wing – directly facing the Kremlin – and succeeded in destroying the sensitive equipment it housed. The wing had over the years been rebuilt with goodness knows what sort of reinforcements, so it must have been one of the most secure of the embassy.

The upshot of all this was that the five of us in the Russian Secretariat now occupied part of the former military suite inside the embassy proper, a section of the original mansion's library, appropriately enough. A gallery under its high ceiling, reached by an iron staircase, housed our collection of old newspapers, while to get to our desks we had to pick our way through heaps more recent newspapers and journals. The Russian Secretariat had succeeded in recreating the cluttered squalor of Research Department, for which I was soon to be roundly ticked off by a visiting FCO inspector.

The ticking off brought home to me for the first time that I was in a position of responsibility. It hadn't seemed like that, since we worked as a 'collective', to use the Soviet term, and had been colleagues back in Research Department. Roy Reeve followed economic affairs. His Russian was by his own admission rather weak, but he had a way with people and quickly got alongside the experts in the US Embassy. Our embassy in turn exploited his talent by making him deputy press officer. Ann Lewis I had known only fleetingly in London, but she had been my fellow teacher in Finland nearly a decade earlier – we had first met on a skiing holiday in Lapland. Ann had stayed on in Finland, where among other things she read the news in English for Finnish radio, endearing herself in this role to my news-hungry father during my parents' 1966 visit. Her knowledge of Finnish was to stand her in good stead in due course. David Miller, who had bridged the gap between Tony Bishop and me in 1965, came out on the same plane as us with his wife Caroline and infant daughter. He was replacing Katherine

Lawrence, who had gone back to England to get married to Roland Smith, one of the chancery officers, a marriage that in those days explicitly precluded her from further work in the diplomatic service. She kindly lent me her car to use while we were waiting for ours to arrive, a mixed blessing as it was an ice blue, low-slung Ford Capri, the only one of its kind in Moscow. To get to it I frequently had to elbow my way through a large crowd of curious onlookers. Finally, we had clerical support from the saturnine John Gibson, who was not a researcher but had worked with us in Research Department and expertly kept the log of the Soviet leaders' movements, as necessary in Moscow as in London.

The focus of our work during the few months when we were all together was the 24th Communist Party Congress, the five-yearly major set piece in the ruling party's calendar. A new five-year economic plan was up for approval and the party's leadership, the 300-odd members of its Central Committee and the dozen or more members of the Politburo, were up for election. As it happened, I had been in Moscow for the previous two congresses, the 22nd in 1961, a momentous affair when Khrushchev finally disposed of Stalin, physically as well as politically – his embalmed body was removed from its position beside Lenin's in the mausoleum on Red Square – and the 23rd in 1966 when the Brezhnev/Kosygin team, having ousted Khrushchev, put forward its policy of economic reform alongside political orthodoxy. That policy had been derailed by the events in Czechoslovakia in 1968, which showed that economic reform – introducing elements of the market into the planned economy and devolving decision-making – inevitably led to a loosening of the Party's tight grip on power. This the Soviet leadership could not contemplate.

There were issues here that would have set the Soviet leaders at loggerheads with each other. Economic reform had been championed by Prime Minister Kosygin. He had shown during the Wilson visit in 1966 that he was a livelier and more trenchant character than his dour public figure suggested. He had been a hit with officials and public alike on his return visit to the UK in February 1967. But Kosygin's star was waning. The death of his wife in May 1968, the comfortable lady who loved to talk about everyday things, may have contributed. But above all Kosygin would have had to accept in the light of Czechoslovakia that economic reform took second place to party control.

Party control was exercised by its General Secretary Brezhnev, the guardian of orthodoxy, both at home and in the socialist camp. A careerist and a vain man, Brezhnev had no real interest in the ideology he espoused. He was engaged in gathering power to himself and using it to promote his image at home and abroad. Despite Czechoslovakia, relations with the West were improving, thanks largely to *Ostpolitik*, the drive by the West German government under Willy Brandt to normalise its relations with the East. The Soviet Union stood to gain by having the West recognise its dominance in Eastern Europe. The process came to be known as *détente*, the relaxation of tension. There was an irritating draw-back for Brezhnev here. Despite being the undisputed Soviet leader, he held no appropriate position in the Soviet state from which he could deal with Western leaders. In deference to the principle of 'collective leadership' the constitution did not provide for an individual to be head of state or president, and Brezhnev spent the next few years working to change it so that he would be able to strut the international stage as he did the domestic one.

Behind these two stood the enigmatic figure of Yuri Andropov, Chairman of the KGB. The restoration of the KGB to its former position of prestige had allowed it to drive with ever increasing speed down a blind alley. Having itself lit the fuse of the dissident movement by over-reacting to the misdemeanours of the writers Sinyavsky and Daniel, it was trying to stop the fire spreading with ever harsher measures against dissidents, even when they were internationally renowned, like the writer Solzhenitsyn. Since the Soviet regime could not admit that the system was anything less than ideal, the only rationale that could be advanced for the repression was that the dissident movement was the tool of evil powers in the West attempting to bring down the Soviet Union. The KGB required the West to be constantly demonised and was thus effectively working against the interests of both Kosygin and Brezhnev as well as against us. There was much discussion in correspondence between the Moscow embassy and the FCO over whether the party and government leaders would bring the KGB to heel, but little expectation that they would, least of all at the set piece occasion we were about to witness.

Nor did they. The congress produced no surprises. The draft five-year plan, which took up the entire issue of *Pravda* one Sunday in mid-February, was a blanket of verbiage. Economic reporting was still nominally in the purview of the embassy's distant commercial section, but the practice of the First Secretary Commercial coming over to brief the rest of us on the economy had lapsed. There wasn't enough substance in the economic debate to divert him from his main job. So analysis of the five-year plan was left to the Russian Secretariat, for which we were poorly qualified. It was my abiding dream to recruit to the Secretariat an academic who could bridge the gap between politics and number crunching. Before long that dream would be realised, though not in the way I had anticipated. Meanwhile, if we couldn't be deep we could at least be quick, so the four of us chopped up the document, read and summarised a section each, then sat round my dining room table over martinis on that Sunday morning and produced a couple of draft reporting telegrams – job done!

The formal part of the Congress, ten days at the end of March, was as dull as we had anticipated. Again, we divided up the reading and analysis of page after page of vacuous speeches and duly summarised and reported them. When the new Politburo was announced, it turned out that everyone was a winner. The existing 11 members were retained and four new ones added. Stability was the order or the day. We duly wrote it all up, and the draft of our main report wound its way upwards without difficulty through the embassy hierarchy. First it went to the Head of Chancery, Ken Scott, experienced and approachable. Then to the Minister, my old boss Joe Dobbs, who had arrived shortly after us for his fourth and last Moscow posting. We had been able to give him, Marie and their four boys a welcome lunch in their former flat, cooked and served by their former maid. The report was finally signed off as a despatch by Sir Duncan Wilson, the ambassador, to whom I felt I owed my posting. He was also informal, approachable and very ready to approve our work.

I did struggle with the specific task Sir Duncan had set me. He wanted a draft despatch that would identify the young technocrats in the communist party who – if they could only gain influence – would lead to a Moscow spring. Having identified them, he wanted to convince Whitehall that it would be more rewarding to nurture them instead of harping on endlessly about the evils of the KGB. In reality, though, the tide of reform was already receding, and even a more dedicated and adventurous spirit than mine would not have been able to identify the people who Sir Duncan was sure could turn it back. But working under Sir Duncan was enjoyable. He and Lady Wilson – a Russian expert in her own right, who was compiling a dictionary together with Professor Akhmanova – frequently invited Raili and me to meals with their Russian guests, cultural figures who featured large in their life.

Sir Duncan was shortly to retire, and while we were there he secured his dream retirement position as Master of Corpus Christi College, Cambridge. When he returned from his successful interview he seemed already to have made the transfer, and among ourselves we wondered whether he would notice the difference at the morning meeting if we called him 'Master' rather than 'Sir'. This was after he had organised his pre-retirement *pièce de résistance* – the Days of British Music in Moscow.

Music was Sir Duncan's passion, and he had extensive contacts among British and Russian musicians. Some years back he had arranged for his daughter Elizabeth to study under the great Russian cellist Mstislav Rostropovich. During our first tour we would occasionally see Elizabeth and her fellow student Jacqueline Du Pré, two willowy, pre-Raphaelite figures, drifting into the embassy to collect mail, while Rostropovich himself would hold up the reception line at the annual Queen's Birthday Party to sing the praises of Sir Duncan to a rather bored Sir Geoffrey Harrison. Rostropovich was a friend of Benjamin Britten, England's foremost composer, and his partner the singer Peter Pears, as was Sir Duncan. With this network in operation an impressive few days of British music-making was set up in Moscow towards the end of April. For me the highlight was a private recital by Pears and Britten in the elegant white room of the residence, in which I was called on to introduce Russian summaries (my own) of Britten's song cycle *Winter Words* to an elite musical audience, including the composer Shostakovich, the pianist Sviatoslav Richter and the ballet dancer Maya Plisetskaya. Rather incongruously, a few days after that I found myself nervously singing in our embassy choir, standing between Sir Duncan and Peter Pears while Britten conducted. Both had been persuaded to lower their standards for an hour or so and generously did so.

On Friday 23rd April, right in the middle of this cultural bonanza, Joe Dobbs was summoned to the Ministry of Foreign Affairs to be told that David Miller had been engaging in activities incompatible with his diplomatic status and should leave the Soviet Union within ten days. He had done no such thing: his expulsion was in retaliation for the Russians being told to withdraw a second secretary from their London embassy. David was the same rank and a suitable target. This was the start of the cycle of expulsions and retaliations that was to dominate our lives for the rest of the year.

It was decided that David and his family would leave as soon as convenient, before news of the expulsion broke, in the hope of allowing them a quiet return to the UK. Raili and I gave a farewell meal for them, ostensibly to celebrate Caroline's birthday, while Ken Scott organised a rather bigger party. It was hard to disguise the real reason for this surge in hospitality, and the Russians themselves seemed to be looking for publicity. They began to leak the story early in the following week, as well as subjecting David to uncomfortably close surveillance, more or less treading on his heels. By the time the Millers reached London the following Wednesday the press were at Heathrow, but were already briefed. The story in *The Times* reflected the UK government's view that the Russians were at fault: their intelligence operations in the UK had reached unacceptable proportions.

Losing David initially left me with one less person in my team, but the office soon gave Katherine Smith, as she now was, dispensation to return to her old job to fill the gap. On a personal level it was a blow. David and I were good friends. We had both been postgraduate students in the Soviet Union and shared the same sort of detached fascination with the country and the foibles of its leaders. Moreover our families lived in the same block; Marjatta frequently baby-sat for the Millers, and they were good to her. So we were all upset.

As if to complement our rather dejected mood, the weather closed in and it snowed on May Day in Moscow that year. But summer came suddenly the following week and our spirits were revived for another couple of months. We spent time at the embassy dacha, had an idyllic picnic in the birch woods north of Moscow, where we were surprised to see elk grazing nearby, and a less idyllic one at Lenin's country house and museum, where our companions were noisy ravens. Raili and I teamed up with another embassy couple to visit Chekhov's country house at Melikhovo, south of Moscow, and I did an official trip to Kiev, capital of the Ukraine (then still just another Soviet Republic), and the Russian provincial towns of Bryansk and Orel (pronounced Oryól). From Orel it was just a taxi ride to a place I had long dreamt of visiting – the country house of Ivan Turgenev, the 19th century writer whom I had studied at Cambridge. The staff at the house remembered a visit from my professor, Lisa Hill, and had on display my supervisor Edward Sands' annotated edition of *Fathers and Sons*. I felt at home there.

Back in Moscow I tried to grow sweet peas up our sunny-side balcony as the Russians did. And we enjoyed an inspired choice for the embassy's amateur dramatics enthusiasts, Peter Ustinov's 1956 play, *Romanoff and Juliet*. This was Shakespeare updated to the Cold War. Roland Smith played the son of the Soviet ambassador to a Central European Ruritania, smitten by love for the American ambassador's daughter and ignoring the advances of the female Soviet sea captain intended for him, who was played by Ann Lewis; while Roy Reeve played the Ruritanian General, a part that Peter Ustinov wrote for himself and to which Roy was perfectly suited. My only contribution was to coach the Embassy's security officer in how to speak English with a Russian accent.

Then on the morning of Monday 21st June Raili picked up the phone in our flat and heard me announce in a rather strangled voice: 'The axe has fallen.' Actually it had fallen late on Friday evening, when poor Joe Dobbs was again summoned to the Ministry of Foreign Affairs to be handed the standard formula, on which the Ministry refused to elaborate, that I and our Assistant Cultural Attaché Patrick Jackson had engaged in activities incompatible with our diplomatic status and had to leave. The embassy hierarchy had kept the news to themselves so as not to spoil our weekends; anyway the clock for the fortnight we were given to pack up and go only started ticking on the Monday.

It had become fairly clear, even after the expulsion of David Miller, that the British would not be budged from their policy of expelling members of the Soviet missions in London when they were caught spying. The Russians for their part had made it clear that they would retaliate, head for head, in every case. So we had good reason to expect that my turn would come some time before the end of my two-year posting. But we were not prepared for it to happen when it did – we had had no inkling of an expulsion in London that might have triggered this response, and we were awaiting a visit from the Permanent Under-Secretary, Sir Denis Greenhill, starting on Tuesday. It turned out that it was only on the Friday that the British government had expelled a First and a Third Secretary from the Soviet Embassy, saying in unusually direct language that they had been 'detected in active intelligence operations against the United Kingdom'. The Russians assumed that the timing had been chosen so that Sir Denis would arrive in Moscow with the score at 2-0 to us, so to speak, and had retaliated that very evening. In fact, as I learnt later, the timing of the Russian spies' expulsions had embarrassed the FCO. The office fully supported the crackdown on Soviet intelligence officers in London but had no control over the actual counter-intelligence operations of MI5. Once presented with the evidence, they had no option but to expel the offending individuals forthwith. By their quick reaction the Russians showed themselves determined to level the score before Sir Denis arrived.

Why Patrick Jackson (a British Council officer) and me? The press quickly noted that we had both been postgraduate students in the Soviet Union, as had the earlier expellee David Miller. There was speculation that we had been chosen because we knew too much about the country. We undoubtedly had fatter KGB files than most, and people like David Miller and me, whose job it was to poke our noses into the recesses of Soviet life, could easily be represented as suspicious characters. I wondered what would come out in the Soviet press. An American colleague with a similar profile to mine, Donald Lesh, had been expelled during our first tour. The Soviet press had concocted an extraordinary mish-mash of fantasies about his activities, including his having made a clandestine trip to Norway allegedly to carry out visual observation of the Soviet/Norwegian border from the Norwegian side, ignoring the fact that he was visiting his Norwegian wife's home village for a holiday. What would they say about our frequent crossings of the Soviet/Finnish border? Nothing, in the event. A long article in *Izvestiya* on 6th August about the nefarious activities of the embassy's Naval Attachés (always fair game) ended lamely by reproducing the official wording on Patrick and me, without any reference to what had been written in the article or what we might have been guilty of. I was disappointed: they could have done better. The mundane reality was that we were on the list of potential expellees (there were others to follow) and our number came up, not least because our ranks (First and Second Secretaries) roughly corresponded to those of the Russians we had kicked out.

There were two things to be sorted out that Monday morning. The Russians took the lead in the first. I was about to make my debut as fully fledged Conference Interpreter at Sir Denis Greenhill's official talks and was on the list of the British delegation that we had given to the Russians. Early on Monday the embassy official looking after the arrangements took a call from the Soviet Ministry of Foreign Affairs asking him to confirm the names of the British delegation, which he did. Later there was another call from the MFA: were we sure that the list was correct? And another: was there not, perhaps, one name too many? And so on, with us refusing to play their game and withdraw me from the delegation. Eventually a call came through at a senior level with the solemn announcement: 'The Soviet Ministry of Foreign Affairs proceeds from the assumption that First Secretary Nicholson will not be part of the British delegation.' We had to acquiesce, but the exchange added an agreeable element of farce to the whole business. Its essence was nicely captured in a *Sydney Morning Herald* cartoon, sent to me by Australian friends a few days later when the affair had become public.

On the second matter I surprised myself by being unusually forceful. I told Ken Scott that I was not going to put up with a repeat of the hugger-mugger way David Miller's expulsion had been handled. It had made his departure a tense and hurried affair, but had succeeded in neither of its objectives: to spare him and his family publicity and to keep down the temperature of Anglo-Soviet relations. We had nothing to hide, and I didn't want to spend the next week or so creeping around as if I had. Ken agreed, but said he would have to get London's permission. I thought we could take the responsibility ourselves and was peeved, but with hindsight I realise

"*We expel two Russian diplomats—they expel two of ours. It's the beginning of a diplomatic dialogue.*"

A cartoon in the Sydney Morning Herald, 26th June 1971 © National Library of Australia

that if the affair was to be made public London needed time to prepare the appropriate parliamentary and press line. Happily, agreement came through, so unlike David we were able to make full use of our fortnight's grace. I arranged for George Walden, the desk officer in London responsible for Anglo-Soviet relations, to ring my parents (whom he had met) to ensure they got the news before it was in the press. We didn't hurry to inform Raili's parents, judging (rightly) that the affair wouldn't make much of a splash in Finland.

With these arrangements in place, we were able to enjoy ourselves before leaving for Finland, where Raili and the children had already planned to spend July, with me joining them at some point. As it was, we could all go together. I apologised rather perfunctorily to my parents that this plan excluded us from making a dramatic entrance into my brother Jonathan's wedding on 26th June. It was to be a small wedding, since Jonathan's bride, like mine, was from abroad, and her family were thinly represented. Originally there had been no question of us making the journey all the way from Moscow. Now we could, but it would have involved losing our fare-paid Finnish holiday. My parents diplomatically put it about that the FCO did not want me back in the UK for a few weeks until the fuss had died down.

I may have been barred from the official part of Sir Denis Greenhill's visit, but the Russians couldn't stop me attending the dinner the ambassador gave Sir Denis and his wife, to which he invited a selection of his musical friends, including David Oistrakh, one of the world's finest violinists, with whom I had a game of croquet on the lawn. Sir Denis was able to sympathise with me, pointing out that as a junior diplomat he had been expelled from Bulgaria, but it hadn't blighted his career, while Joe Dobbs put a fatherly arm round my shoulder and said he was sure I'd get back to Moscow some time. In fact, getting back to Moscow wasn't a question that concerned me at the time. It had been a packed six months and I was actually quite happy to take a rest from Russian affairs. David Miller had the same sort of feeling after his expulsion and was thinking of looking for a posting in Eastern Europe.

The British press carried the expulsion story on Wednesday 23rd June, where it became entangled with the story of the defection of a Soviet engineer at the Paris air show that was actually unrelated.

DAILY EXPRESS

No. 22,090   WEDNESDAY JUNE 23 1971   Weather: Mainly dry, sunny spells   Price 3p

As FO chief flies to Russia

TIT-FOR-TAT SPY ROW

Out Two Britons from Moscow

Out Two Russians from London

By DANIEL McGEACHIE

AN amazing diplomatic row between Britain, Russia, and France blew up last night, coinciding with the defection of mystery man Anatol Fedosseiev.

As *Foreign Office* chief Sir Denis Greenhill flew off to Moscow on a "good will" visit:—

BRITAIN ordered out two men in the Soviet Embassy in London who "had been detected in active intelligence operations against the U.K."

RUSSIA promptly tit-for-tatted by expelling two British Embassy men from Moscow for "activities incompatible with their diplomatic status."

FRANCE accused Britain of "deception" over Fedosseiev—who, it was thought, has been in British hands three weeks.

How the press covered the expulsion, with the author in small print, below

Sir Denis Greenhill, who as a junior diplomat in 1949 was thrown out of Bulgaria, will now as Permanent Under-Secretary have a tough job sorting it all out in Moscow.

It was last Friday that First Secretary Lev Sherstnev and Third Secretary Valery Chousovitin, of Russia's London Embassy, were given two weeks to leave because of their "intelligence operations."

On Monday Russia gave two weeks' notice to quit to our men in Moscow, Mr. Martin Nicholson, 33, head of the secretariat since last December, and Mr. Patrick Jackson, 30, the assistant cultural attaché, because of their "activities."

Both are married with families in Moscow and speak Russian fluently.

Now that it was public we were inundated with invitations to farewell dinners, which for once I enjoyed, knowing this would be my last fling in the world of diplomatic entertaining for some time. Wherever we went we had more than the usual complement of surveillance cars on our tail, but I was used to that and only felt ill at ease on one occasion, when driving to a dinner given by David Bonavia, correspondent of *The Times*. Suddenly I realised that we had no car on our tail at all and thought rather illogically that we might have lost our way and would find 'our' car waiting for us when we arrived. My colleague Patrick Jackson was less experienced and more excited by the attention that was being devoted to him. He took to playing with his surveillance team by executing unexpected manoeuvres, until one evening as he returned from a dinner his car seized up, smoke pouring from the bonnet. The cooling system had been emptied by the KGB, a gentle reminder that it was they who held the whip hand.

We were also followed when we were out on foot; even Marjatta and the children had their own team when they went out without Raili and me. But the surveillance was not designed to intimidate and was quite different from what David Miller had experienced and from what was to come later in the year. It even had its comic moments. Our followers were naturally behind us most of the time; one sensed them rather than saw them. But once when we were walking with the children on the Lenin Hills we spotted a young couple ahead of us sitting on the grass; instinct told us they were part of the team and were probably there to take a family photograph. As we approached they fell into a passionate embrace so that we couldn't see their faces. Our instinct had been right: in the prim Moscow of those days nobody would be seen kissing in public. The 'loving couple' remained among our Moscow stories for many years after that. The only time I came into physical contact with my 'tail' was assuredly an accident. We always bought our bread from a shop round the corner, and one evening, precisely at closing time, we noticed we had run out. I dashed out of the flat, ran down the street, rounded the corner and just made it to the bread shop. I was sauntering back round the same corner with the loaf under my arm when – smack! – a young man ran straight into me, sending us both sprawling. Picking ourselves up, we exchanged shy grins and continued on our separate ways, he doubtless to interrogate the shop assistants as to what I had been up to while out of sight. Once again, nobody ever ran in the streets of Moscow, and I knew that this was my 'tail', who must have assumed I was deliberately trying to give him the slip with my hasty, unannounced flight from our flat.

Why was the KGB expending so many resources on us? It was common knowledge that they tended to increase surveillance over the last six months of a diplomat's posting; I had experienced this at the end of my first tour. Now my last six months were being compressed into a couple of weeks; did they have to compress their six months' surveillance plan into two weeks? Or did they really think that, despite the lack of evidence, I was running agents? In that case my unexpected departure might drive me to take risks in order to contact them before I left. But Marjatta and the children? Many years later, as a fuller story emerged of how the Soviet agent Oleg Penkovsky was run from the British Embassy in Moscow, it transpired that one of his points of contact was Janet Chisholm, wife of the embassy visa officer, as she played with her children in a park. So keeping an eye on our nanny and children was not entirely irrational either.

Happily, we were not distracted by these things, as we had enough to do to ourselves. Raili and the children took the whole episode in their stride, although Karin was upset at losing her friend Patrick, the son of the Reuters bureau chief Andrew Waller. Patrick, though, was even more upset. When he had been told we were leaving he was found in floods of tears long after he should have been asleep. Colin was recovering from a high fever with convulsions, which had worried us far more than the expulsion, but he was well enough to continue with the adventurous outings Marjatta and her fellow nanny organised, including a hydrofoil trip on the Moscow River.

Friday 2nd July was the only dark day. Two days earlier, the three-man crew of the Soviet space ship *Soyuz 11*, who had spent a record 23 days in orbit, were found dead on landing – a faulty seal as they were transferring to their landing capsule had led to a momentary decompression, enough to kill them instantly. All Moscow came to a standstill on that Friday for their funeral, a rare occasion when public and official grief coincided. We too were affected by the mood, as our busy ring road fell eerily silent. But the funeral affected us more directly. I had just realised with sinking heart that while I and my family, with our diplomatic visas, were free to travel out of the Soviet Union however and whenever we chose, Marjatta had to get a stamp in her passport from OVIR, the Department of Visas and Registrations, and I had done nothing about it. She was due to travel with us the next day, but without this stamp she would be tipped out of the train before the Finnish border, and we couldn't let that happen. I charged Sasha, the principal 'fixer' in the Russian Admin, with getting to OVIR and coming back with Marjatta's passport stamped that very day, come what may. But I feared all along that he wouldn't even get to the OVIR office through shutdown Moscow, let alone persuade the notoriously obstructive bureaucrats there to issue the stamp. Great was my relief, therefore, when later in the day he appeared, stamped passport in hand. He and his driver knew all the back streets and had got to the office without difficulty, where he had gone straight to the director. 'I have my secret weapon that opens all doors,' he said, flashing his gap-toothed smile. What was it? A *Beautiful Britain* calendar, issued by the Central Office of Information, which he had presented to the delighted director. The innocence of those days, when the favours of a Russian official could be so simply obtained!

So the next day, Saturday 3rd July, we were able to set off in good spirits. It was Karin's sixth birthday. We had promised her a joint birthday celebration along with Colin in August, but with our train only leaving towards midnight, the Wallers found time to throw a surprise birthday party for her, to which Colin was invited, leaving Raili and me to make our final preparations. Another surprise awaited us at the station – 26 colleagues and friends (as I recorded in a letter to my parents), their numbers swelled by their KGB 'tails', were on hand to see us off, with four bottles of champagne, the corks flying over the top of the carriage. As the train started to trundle off into the night, the courteous old steward handed us our glasses of tea, commenting: 'They gave you a good send off!' It was to be 17 years before I returned to the Soviet Union.

We had a good reception in Lahti as well, when we arrived the following day – with Raili's home in Artjärvi as our destination we didn't need to go all the way to Helsinki. True, it wasn't the press, cameras flashing, as my Walter Mitty self would rather have liked, but two dignified Finnish gentlemen, identically dressed. They were Raili's father and Jaakko Koivu, the taxi driver whose father had made the handsome twill suits that each was wearing. An hour or so later we spilled out of the taxi into the lakeside cabin that Raili's father had secured for us, and from there straight into the lake on a perfect summer's day.

We quickly settled into Finnish holiday mode, with Raili doing most of the socialising and me rather more of the child-minding than I was used to, as Marjatta took stock of her situation before returning to Moscow to take up another nanny post in an embassy family with five children. The only thing I missed was the drinking session with the packers that I had enjoyed at the end of our first tour (we had left the packing to others after our departure), so I deliberately drank myself silly one night in our little cabin after sauna. Perhaps the strain had been greater than I realised.

Back in England a month later we were able to walk straight into our house, our reluctant tenant having just moved out. We soon got into our stride, thanks to my parents looking after most of our administrative arrangements. But not only they – the head teacher of Orleans Infants School had on her own initiative re-registered Karin as soon as she saw the news of our expulsion in the press.

Nor was I short of work at the office, filling in from London the gaps in the reporting of the Russian Secretariat, now reduced in size. It was here that I read one of the ambassador's final despatches before his retirement: the particular task he had set me when I arrived and which I had left for others to complete. Ponderously titled *The Two Cultures in Soviet Life: 'Red' and, or versus 'Expert'*, it posited the thesis that the Communist Party was open to reform. The Soviet leaders needed the benefits of advanced, Western technology but were unwilling to pay the price of ideological relaxation that would allow the free exchange of scientific ideas. Such freedom carried the risk that Soviet society might be infected with Western values. So to maintain control they would have to allow the party itself to become less dogmatic and more technically minded. Out of self interest, he argued, the rising generation might become more rational. This was the optimistic thesis that Sir Duncan had been so anxious to prove throughout his tour and to which he had harnessed me. Try as I did, I had never been able to find the evidence to support it, and as I read the despatch that had finally emerged I suspected that Sir Duncan's heart was no longer in it. What I didn't know was that Sir Duncan was at the same time arguing on the same grounds for a less confrontational solution to the problem of Soviet intelligence activities in the UK. His arguments cut no ice. It was painfully clear that his judgment had been affected by his almost exclusive involvement with the musical world, an unrepresentative segment of society in the Soviet Union as anywhere else.

That summer, despite the clouds hanging over Anglo-Soviet relations, the process of *détente* was moving slowly forward. A key element, the Quadripartite Agreement on Berlin between the four occupying powers (the Soviet Union, the United States of America, Britain and France), was about to fall into place. Tony Bishop had been going back and forth for many months, interpreting, but it was time for him to have a holiday, so he suggested I should take over for the last session. All that was left, in fact, was the proof-reading of the Russian text of the agreement. I jumped at the idea of a visit to West Berlin.

The agreement was not designed to alter the status of West Berlin – a Western enclave in the middle of Communist East Germany – but to put in place practical measures that would reduce the chronic tensions that afflicted this neuralgic point between East and West. But each side suspected the other of being prepared to use the agreement to further its own aims – the Russians to detach West Berlin from the West, and in particular the Federal Republic of Germany; the Western allies to cement its position as a de facto extension of the FRG. The latent divisions on this issue were exposed when we came to compare the final texts of the agreement. Oddly enough, although neither East nor West Germany was a party to the agreement, the negotiations had been carried out in German, the *lingua franca* of the four occupying powers, with English being the working language of the agreed text. So it was late in the day when the Russian text was produced, and I was in Berlin to examine it. On this contentious issue the English text (to which the Russians had agreed) bridged the gap by stating that 'The Western Sectors of Berlin continue not to be a constituent part of the FRG'. As with many international agreements, each side drew what it wanted from the formulation – the West emphasised the word 'continue'; the Russians the word 'not'. But the Russian text that was presented to us sounded as if it meant 'henceforth will not be ...' i.e. a change of status. Told that this was unacceptable, the Russians were aghast. There was only a day to go before signature. This was the text that had Foreign Minister Gromyko's approval, and could not be changed. It was just a question of style – the Russian 'henceforth' was qualified by 'and', they tried to persuade us, which gave it the meaning of 'henceforth as now'.

I was despatched back to London early the next morning to show the texts to Tom Brimelow as the Deputy Under-Secretary supervising the negotiations, and he was adamant. He agreed that 'continue not to be' was ugly in either language, but it said what we wanted to say. The Russian wording might be elegant, but it was open to misrepresentation. The Russians eventually conceded the point, and the final Russian wording, using the words 'as before' met our requirement. But signature was delayed, and the magnificent banquet laid on by the French (it was their turn to be the hosts at the Allied Control Commission's headquarters in Berlin) remained uneaten, at least by the official negotiators.

Although I didn't know it at the time, the signing of the Quadripartite Agreement on 3rd September removed the last obstacle in the way of a long-planned operation to expel a large number of Soviet spies from London and thus bring an end to the war of attrition that we couldn't win.

When I came into work on Friday 24th September 1971, I was summoned to see Julian Bullard, Head of Northern Department. Handing me a collection of papers, he told me that this was operation FOOT (he apologised for the banal code name) – the summary expulsion of no fewer than 105 officials from the Soviet Embassy and Soviet Trade Delegation, more than the entire staff of the British Embassy in Moscow. It was going into action that very afternoon. He wanted me to read and mentally translate into Russian the *aide-mémoire* that the Permanent Under-Secretary, Sir Denis Greenhill, would read out and hand over the Soviet Chargé d'Affaires, Ivan Ippolitov, along with the list of the 105. I was to sit in and be prepared to put it into Russian in case Ippolitov didn't understand, or affected not to understand, what it was all about. There was an important point to be got across: ceilings would be set on the number of personnel in Soviet organisations at their post-expulsion level. If it were necessary to expel anyone after that, the ceiling on the organisation they came from would be reduced by one. The principle of the 'falling ceiling', as it came to be known in the department, was of course, designed to make the Russians watch their step in the future. Ippolitov also had to understand why there were in fact two lists: one consisted of 90 officials currently in the UK; the other of 15 who were not at the moment in the UK but held valid re-entry visas. They would not be allowed to return.

I mugged up on the documents on the spot, as Julian would not let me take them out of his office, or indeed breathe a word to anyone about what was about to happen. The reason was simply that although long in the planning, the date of the expulsions had been postponed several times. It was not a case of over-cautious officials, Julian emphasised – the FCO was solidly in favour of the action – but of government ministers getting cold feet, and this could happen right up to the moment action was taken.

Julian passed me over to George Walden to elaborate. He said that the Russians had been given every opportunity to respond to the hints we had repeatedly dropped that we were not expecting them to abandon entirely their intelligence-gathering activity, but to reduce its scale and be a little less brazen about it all. But the Soviet Foreign Minister Gromyko had not even replied to the latest letters from our Secretary of State, Sir Alec Douglas-Home. This was of course the ultimate discourtesy to a gentleman of Sir Alec's stamp, and he had been incensed. After a series of cabinet level discussion, Ministers had finally agreed that there was no alternative but to wield a big stick. With the Berlin agreement now signed, the Russian reactions were unlikely to upset the *détente* applecart, and a date had been fixed for mid-October.

But things had changed again. On 3rd September, the very day the Berlin Agreement was signed, Oleg Lyalin, a KGB specialist in sabotage masquerading as a knitwear representative in the Soviet Trade Delegation, had put himself in the hands of the British authorities. He had been secretly co-operating with MI5 for some months, but had recently been arrested for drunken driving. He was ordered home by his Soviet boss, but instead defected, bringing with him documents that showed what he had been up to. It was only a matter of time before his activities became public knowledge, and the government would be asked what it was doing about this state of affairs. Better to act first, so operation FOOT was brought forward to September.

At the appointed time I was sitting beside Sir Denis Greenhill as he read out the charge sheet in his monotonous, gravelly voice to the Soviet Chargé. I didn't think Ippolitov was taking it in, as he was nervously leafing through the list of expellees that had already been handed to him – it was typed in triple spacing and went on for page after page. So I was prepared to do my bit when Sir Denis had finished reading and said to the Chargé: 'If there's anything you've found difficult to understand, Mr Ippolitov, I have Mr Nicholson here to repeat it in Russian.' But it wasn't necessary. 'No, no,' replied Ippolitov in a husky voice. 'All is clear. Very drastic measures, Sir Greenhill, very drastic!' And with a few standard courtesies he was shown out. If he had taken his eyes off that list on his return journey and looked out of the car window he would have seen that the billboards for the evening newspapers were already announcing KGB OUT! Having decided to go the whole hog with the expulsions, the government had arranged publicity to match.

I didn't fully share the sense of triumph, verging on triumphalism, that pervaded the office once the deed was done. At a personal level I had doubtless looked smug when Sir Denis read out the sentence of the *aide-mémoire* that referred to 'unjustified acts of Soviet retaliation such as the recent expulsions of Mr Miller, Mr Nicholson and Mr Jackson' as factors contributing to the government's decision to act. But it was not a case of 'sweet revenge'. I had never taken my expulsion as directed personally at me; I was simply one of the pawns that had been exchanged in the course of the game whose end we were now reaching. But along with my Research Department colleagues I was anxious about the inevitable Soviet retaliation – it was bound to affect us.

And so it did. On 8th October, after two miserable weeks in which the KGB, now angry, harassed the embassy staff, the Soviet First Deputy Foreign Minister summoned our new ambassador Sir John Killick to tell him that as well as cancelling a number of high level visits and meetings the Russians were expelling four members of the embassy and one resident businessman. They were also cancelling the valid return visas of three other Moscow-resident businessmen and would deny visas to ten former members of the Embassy, should they ever apply. So there were 18 names in all, the selection clearly intended to mirror as best it could the spread of our expulsions, with the businessmen, former members of the embassy's Commercial Department and science attachés being deemed the equivalents of members of the Soviet Trade Delegation in London.

The Soviet counter-measures fell far short of London's worst fears and were greeted with relief. We had put the Russians on the spot: they couldn't retaliate for the 105 with head for head expulsions. To do so would destroy our Moscow embassy and would effectively lead to a break in diplomatic relations. This the Russians didn't want to do – they gained more from their presence in the open society of London than we did in the closed society of Moscow – so for the sake of appearances they bulked up the numbers of expellees with an assortment of 'also-rans'.

But the Russian Secretariat, actual and potential, was hit disproportionally hard. We in Research Department bridled somewhat at Sir John Killick's blithe comment that the embassy had 'got off very lightly indeed'. Of the four embassy expellees, two were from the Secretariat: Ann Lewis, who had been on the point of extending her tour for a further year; and Dr Philip Hanson, a distinguished economist from Birmingham University, who had been in his post as Roy Reeve's replacement for a matter of weeks only. Expulsion was particularly hard on him since he had obtained leave of absence from his university in the expectation of spending a year in Moscow and had uprooted his family, who were not conditioned, as we were, to frequent moves. I felt bad about his expulsion, since he was the man I had dreamt of earlier in the year when struggling to analyse the Soviet five-year plan: the academic who could bridge the gap between politics and number crunching; and I had been in part responsible for his appointment. I had hosted Phil on a reconnaissance visit to Moscow in early summer and had been looking forward to working with him. I was no longer there

The four embassy staff expellees pose outside the Embassy shortly after the announcement.
From the left: Alan Holmes, Head of Registry; Ann Lewis, Russian Secretariat; Philip Hanson,
Russian Secretariat; Tony Wolstenholme, Assistant Naval Attaché.
Courtesy of Philip Hanson

when he arrived, and now nor was he. He worked out the rest of his FCO contract in Research Department, then returned to Birmingham, though it was years before he got back to the Soviet Union.

An even more distinguished economist, Professor Alec Nove of Glasgow University, featured among the also-rans, perhaps because after the war he had worked in the Board of Trade and done a stint in the Moscow embassy. The inclusion in the list of a senior academic with an international reputation was a crass misjudgement by its compilers: it ensured that the list wouldn't be taken seriously even by those who might otherwise have thought 'there must be something in it'. But it had to be taken seriously by those affected, among them our former Research Department colleague Ray Hutchings, another economist, who had left a few years back to pursue an academic career that didn't prosper. He made a rather precarious living as a peripatetic lecturer and was upset by his inclusion on the list, which he felt might damage his reputation as well as his ability to top up his knowledge by occasional visits to the Soviet Union. He wrote to the office to appeal for some sort of financial compensation, but was told – rather callously, I thought – that he'd come to the wrong address, since it was the Russians who had been the cause of his misfortune. The list also included Bob Longmire, my predecessor as Head of the Russian Secretariat, who was not likely to have done another posting, and – distressingly for all of us – Geoff Murrell, who certainly would, most probably as my successor. Psychologically it was more of a blow for him, taken by stealth, as it were, as he dug his garden on that Saturday morning in October, than it had been for me, shot down in battle.

The Soviet reprisals left Katherine Smith as the 'last man standing' in the Russian Secretariat. David Bonavia was right to report in *The Times* on 11th October that the 'main effect of the expulsions and bannings is to cripple the work of the Secretariat'. True, it was gradually revived as the internal political section of Chancery, but its historic title was allowed to lapse, and the brand, as we would say today, was lost. Rightly or wrongly, it was deemed to attract too much attention of the wrong sort.

Overall, however, operation FOOT was a resounding success. It was well received by the UK's friends and allies, who were given the unpublished list of the 105 and in many cases refused visas to our expellees when they sought new territories for their operations, thus compounding the KGB's misery. The exception were the French, who were currently raising their allies' eyebrows by hosting Soviet Communist Party leader Leonid Brezhnev on what was effectively a state visit; they dismissed the episode as 'a traffic accident'.

There had been some overkill. Many years later a Russian diplomat, with no axe of his own to grind, assured me that among the 105 there were genuine diplomats, friends of his, who had unfairly been lumped in with the intelligence officials. I believed him, but as Stalin is reputed to have said when confronted with the number of innocent people carried off in his purges: 'When you cut down a forest, the splinters fly!' The extent of the damage to the

UK's security wreaked by these people was also debatable. Thought had been given to bolstering our case by publishing some of the documents Lyalin had brought with him. They showed that he had been reconnoitring the Yorkshire coast as a possible landing point for sabotage teams. But wiser counsels had prevailed. Lyalin's tips to future Soviet agents about how to look inconspicuous in a Yorkshire pub would be just as likely to raise a laugh with the sceptical British public as to fill them with indignation.

But the point was not so much what they had been up to, as the way they had been doing it – swamping MI5's efforts to keep track of them by sheer numbers and brazenly evading all our attempts to keep a lid on those numbers. There had been a 'ceiling' on numbers in the Soviet Embassy for several years, which they evaded by expanding the Trade Delegation, and when a ceiling was put on that they increased the number of 'working wives'. Although it didn't figure on the charge sheet, the unequal exchange of Gerald Brooke for the Krogers that the previous, Labour government had eventually been forced to concede in 1969, had added to our humiliation. The Russians, in short, were making fools of us and needed a sharp rap on the knuckles, which only a major expulsion could provide.

It was a Conservative government, in office for only a year, that delivered the rap, and the Soviet press not surprisingly attributed it to the diehard anti-Sovietism of the Tories. In fact, as Julian Bullard had intimated to me, it was the steely FCO team – Greenhill, Brimelow, Walden and himself – who had consistently advocated major surgery. They were not Cold War warriors, but their considerable collective experience of dealing with the Russians told them that nothing less would do the trick. The Cabinet, as we can now see from the most recent examination of the decision by the former FCO historian Gill Bennett, was constantly searching for less 'drastic measures' – a negotiated staged withdrawal without publicity, for example – and was worried up to the last moment about Soviet reprisals.[2]

Had the Russians looked carefully at Sir Alec Douglas-Home's many letters to Gromyko they would have seen an 'invitation to dance'. Perhaps Gromyko did advocate a more subtle response but, as we Kremlinologists had always pointed out, the most senior Soviet minister that our government dealt with regularly at that time wasn't even a member of the Politburo, the Soviet equivalent of our Cabinet. Gromyko had to play the hand he was dealt by the policy makers, the Party leaders and the KGB, and it gave him no room for flexibility. The irony of this was that by its unwillingness to play the diplomatic game the KGB cooked its own goose.

Meanwhile, we expellees found our various ways forward. Ann Lewis and David Miller more or less left Research Department. Ann went on to postings in Helsinki and East Berlin, interspersed with a stint in the Cabinet Office and ending her career as Head of the FCO's Cultural Relations Department. David left for Berlin, Belgrade and the NATO Secretariat, also with a stint in the Cabinet

---

[2] Gill Bennett, *Six Moments of Crisis*, London 2013

Office, ending his career as ambassador to the new, post-Soviet Republic of Armenia. Geoff Murrell also had a posting to Belgrade and despite his 1971 banning secured two further postings to Moscow, where I replaced him as Minister Counsellor on his retirement in 1994.

But before that I had also done my share of wandering – a decade with Central Europe as its focus. After my expulsion from Moscow, Ted Orchard outlined three possible courses for me. The first was to stay put in Research Department, where with the embassy unable to provide a full reporting service there was plenty of work to do. I could continue interpreting as and when the opportunity arose. But with Anglo-Soviet relations in the doldrums, the opportunity for high level interpreting would be limited for the foreseeable future, and Tony Bishop in any case now had the inside track. The idea of having two Conference Interpreters in Russian sitting in London, neither of whom could get to Moscow (Tony having been expelled in 1965), was anyway a bit ludicrous. The second option was to transfer to the Branch A of the Diplomatic Service. A 'fast track' competition for selected Branch B officers would soon take place. Success would guarantee me a good career if I were prepared to serve anywhere in the world and tackle any subject that came up. I had never been much interested in travel for its own sake or in the art of diplomacy as such and entered the competition without much enthusiasm. I was turned down, quite rightly, for lack of motivation. The third option was to replace my Research Department colleague Joe Banks in Prague, where he operated as a one-man 'Czech

Secretariat'. This was more my sort of thing. I relished the idea of learning another Slavonic language, but was apprehensive about turning up as an expert in a country about which I knew very little. I was persuaded, however, that my knowledge of the way Communist systems worked would put me well ahead of most, and my knowledge of the Soviet Union in particular would come in handy now that, after the heady days of 1968, Czechoslovakia was once again under the Soviet boot.

So 1971 ended with us preparing to move once again – and once again looking wistfully at the settled lives of our neighbours in our tranquil close.